Language Arts Curriculum Team

WORDSMITHING
A SPELLING PROGRAM FOR GRADES 3–8

ARDY SMITH

ANNE DAVIES

Wordsmithing*: A Spelling Program for Grades 3–8

* Smith: one who creates [Old English]
Wordsmith: one who finds joy in creation of words

PEGUIS PUBLISHERS
WINNIPEG • CANADA

© 1996 by Ardy Smith and Anne Davies

All rights reserved. Except as noted, no part of this publication may be reproduced or transmitted in any form or by any means—graphic, electronic, or mechanical—without prior written permission of the publisher. Any request to photocopy any part of this book, other than pages where permission to reproduce is stated, shall be directed in writing to the Canadian Reprography Collective, 379 Adelaide Street W., Ste. M1, Toronto, ON   M5V 1S5.

Printed and bound in Canada by Hignell Printing Limited

96   97   98   99   00   5   4   3   2   1

Canadian Cataloguing in Publication Data

Smith, Ardys Lee, 1951–

   Wordsmithing, a spelling program for grades 3–8

   ISBN 1-895411-85-8

1. English language – Orthography and spelling – Study and teaching (Elementary)   I. Davies, Anne, 1955–   II. Title.

LB1574.S48 1996   372.6'32   C96-920157-5

Book and cover design: Laura Ayers

Peguis Publishers Limited
100–318 McDermot Avenue
Winnipeg, Manitoba
Canada   R3A 0A2
1-800-667-9673

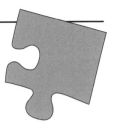

To all the artists, musicians, athletes, inventors, scientists, and authors who couldn't spell and who, in spite of that, enriched our world in so many ways; and to all the children who will enrich our future.

CONTENTS

ACKNOWLEDGMENTS ix

INTRODUCTION 1
  WHO IS THIS BOOK FOR? 1
  HOW DO CHILDREN LEARN TO SPELL? 2
  HOW IS THIS BOOK DIFFERENT FROM OTHER SPELLING BOOKS AND PROGRAMS? 3
  KEY POINTS FOR WORDSMITHING 4
  OVERVIEW OF THE PROGRAM 5
  SUMMARY 6

1. MONDAY: COLLECTING THE WORDS 7
  KEY POINTS FOR MONDAY 8
  MONDAY IDEAS:
    SPELLING SPINES 10
    WORD FAMILY TREES 11
    THE SECRET OF NYMS 13
    CONTRACTIONS, COMPOUNDS, AND CONUNDRUMS 14
    QUICK FIXES 15
    SOUNDS LIKE/LOOKS LIKE 16
    ENVIROPRINT 18
  SUMMARY 19
  PERSONAL FAVORITES, NEW AND OLD 20

2. TUESDAY: TAKING A CLOSER LOOK 23
  KEY POINTS FOR TUESDAY 23
  TUESDAY IDEAS:
    BEGINNING, ENDING, MIDDLE 24
    WORD PARTS 26
    HAPPY ENDINGS 27
    MISTAKES AND MISDEMEANORS 29
    HIGHLIGHTS 30
  SUMMARY 30
  PERSONAL FAVORITES, NEW AND OLD 31

Contents v

3. WEDNESDAY: MAKING SENSE OF WORDS   33
KEY POINTS FOR WEDNESDAY   33
WEDNESDAY IDEAS:
- NOISY MNEMONICS   34
- LOOKS LIKE/SOUNDS LIKE   35
- WORD ORIGINS   36
- THESAURUS REX   37
- CLUES   38
- INVENTIONS   39

SUMMARY   40
PERSONAL FAVORITES, NEW AND OLD   41

4. THURSDAY: PLAYING WITH WORDS   43
KEY POINTS FOR THURSDAY   43
THURSDAY IDEAS:
- TWENTY WORD QUESTIONS   44
- THE DICTIONARY GAME   46
- SPELLING-CLUE COUNTDOWN   47
- MYSTERY PICTURES   48
- CLASS PUZZLES   49
- GAME OVER   50
- COMMERCIALLY PRODUCED WORD GAMES   51

SUMMARY   51
PERSONAL FAVORITES, NEW AND OLD   52

5. FRIDAY: SHOWING WHAT WE KNOW   55
KEY POINTS FOR FRIDAY   55
FRIDAY IDEAS:
- WORD BEES   56
- PEER TESTS   57
- TRANSFER TALLY   58
- PROVE IT!   59
- SELF-REPORTS   60

SUMMARY   61
PERSONAL FAVORITES, NEW AND OLD   62

6. CLASSROOM ROUTINES THAT SUPPORT YOUR SPELLING PROGRAM   65
KEY POINTS FOR CLASSROOM ROUTINES   65
IDEAS FOR CLASSROOM ROUTINES:
- ONGOING ASSESSMENT   66
  - *APPLICATION OF SPELLING SKILLS*   66
  - *ERROR ANALYSIS*   67
  - *ABILITY TO SELF-CORRECT*   68
  - *REPEATED SPELLING TEST*   69
- WRITING PROCESS   70

    PROOFREADING   71
    WEEKLY EDIT   73
    MYSTERY MESSAGES/ C.O.P.S./ DAILY EDITS   74
    MORNING NEWS   76
    CALENDAR TIME   77
    PASSWORD OUT THE DOOR   78
    WEIRD WORD COLLECTION   78
SUMMARY   79
PERSONAL FAVORITES, NEW AND OLD   80

7. EVALUATION   83
    KEY POINTS FOR EVALUATION   84
EVALUATION IDEAS:
    WAYS TO COLLECT AND ORGANIZE SPELLING DATA   85
    SPELLING ANALYSIS   86
    REFLECTING ON LEARNING   88
    SETTING CRITERIA   90
    STRATEGIES GOOD SPELLERS USE   91
SUMMARY   91
PERSONAL FAVORITES, NEW AND OLD   92

8. INVITING, INCLUDING, AND INFORMING OTHERS   95
    KEY POINTS FOR INVITING, INCLUDING, AND INFORMING OTHERS   95
IDEAS FOR INVITING, INCLUDING, AND INFORMING OTHERS:
    HELPING PARENTS HELP WITH SPELLING HOMEWORK   96
    SPELL-A-BRATION   97
    SPELLING GAMES FAMILY NIGHT   98
    SPELLING NEWSLETTERS   101
SUMMARY   102
PERSONAL FAVORITES, NEW AND OLD   103

9. QUESTIONS PARENTS AND TEACHERS ASK   105

CONCLUSION   111

APPENDIX: BLACKLINE MASTERS   113

BIBLIOGRAPHY   132

**TEACHER REFERENCE LIST
    OF SOME COMMON SPELLING PATTERNS**   134

ACKNOWLEDGMENTS

We would like to thank the following people for their contributions, through good company and great conversation, to our writing: Neill Dixon, Kathleen Gregory, and Colleen Politano. A special thank you to Caren Cameron who took time to read and respond to earlier drafts of this manuscript; she helped us find the book amongst the words. We have appreciated the good company, good food, and great accommodations Gayle Sams of the Sea provided to us during our intensive writing periods. We'd especially like to thank Patsy for her wonderful raisin bread! It sustained us through some difficult moments. We'd like to acknowledge the wonderful work of Daphne Louis and Terry Johnson and thank them for the idea behind "Spelling Clue Countdown" in Chapter 4. Once more, Annalee Greenberg, our editor, has done a marvelous job taming the unruly words we sent her way. Thank you, Annalee. And to Laura Ayers, who has helped us create books that are teacher-friendly in their design, we appreciate your talent and hard work. We'd also like to acknowledge the ongoing support of everyone at Peguis Publishers, who directly and indirectly help make our writing life wonderful.

INTRODUCTION

WHO IS THIS BOOK FOR?

Wordsmithing: A Spelling Program for Grades 3–8, the fourth book in the Building Connections series, is intended for busy elementary teachers (grade three and up) who are trying to make sense of the many changes taking place in education today. Take the process approach to writing. Add language across the curriculum, self-esteem building, making learning relevant. Then incorporate parent's concern over "standards" into the mix—the result can be a recipe for confusion. Many of us are left wondering about where spelling instruction fits in or if spelling even counts. This book can serve as a starting point for teachers who believe, as we do, that spelling *does* count, but spelling instruction as we know it doesn't always make sense within the current mix of language arts practices. This book is designed to help teachers and their students make sense of spelling. It includes

- a weekly spelling program with daily activities
- numerous classroom routines you can incorporate to support spelling
- specific ways parents can support spelling development at home
- evaluation strategies
- answers to questions teachers and parents frequently ask

This program requires that you, as teacher, determine the activities and strategies most appropriate for your students. Depending on your choices, this could result in over one hundred different spelling-program weeks. In combination with all the word collections you and your students will develop, this program becomes a spelling program with infinite variety. Wordsmithing—spelling and word play—is a lifelong activity.

HOW DO CHILDREN LEARN TO SPELL?

We often wonder why some of our best and brightest students are not good spellers, even though they have had the same instructional experiences and opportunities as the rest of the class. Research over the past few years has shown that learning to spell is, like learning to speak, a developmental process. It has also indicated that good spellers and unexpectedly poor spellers differ in their general cognitive processing styles (Frith 1980; Gentry 1987; Harste, Burke, and Woodward 1983; Henderson and Beers 1980; Smith 1992).

Most children rely on a sounding-out strategy during the primary years—the strategy most available to them at their stage of cognitive development. At around the age of ten, most people begin to shift to visual and orthographic strategies. These are based on how a word looks and how it is likely to be spelled given how similar words are spelled. This occurs because, for many children, changes in cognitive development allow for storage of the visual representations of words. As children become exposed to more and more words through their reading and writing, they are supported in this shift to more effective spelling strategies.

Not all learners make this shift, though, and some make it later than others. Some researchers have suggested that anywhere from 5 percent to 20 percent of the normally functioning population with average and above-average intelligence continue to be nonspellers throughout their adulthood. There is some evidence that these unexpectedly poor spellers process information simultaneously or *holistically* while good spellers tend to process information *sequentially*. Readers who process holistically absorb larger meanings, without attending to the discrete units we call words, thus not noticing their makeup. This interferes with the development of a visual store of words.

Many inventors, scientists, authors, musicians, artists, actors, and athletes have been poor at spelling. It is important to remember this; often students' achievements have been inadvertently hindered by making spelling count when it shouldn't. If a child is gifted in sciences, it is not acceptable to give her an average or low mark because "points were taken off for spelling." If a student can't spell, it means only one thing—that the student can't spell. It doesn't mean that she is lazy, stupid, or didn't know the content. It shouldn't mean that she is blocked from succeeding in other areas of study.

The view of correct spelling as a key indicator of intelligence and success—and poor spelling as a sign of laziness, stupidity, or willful disregard for adult conventions—pervades society at large. People cringe when they see misspelled words on signs, menus, or posters. Parents become concerned when they see misspelled words on children's schoolwork, and often blame teachers, falling standards, and lack of emphasis on spelling in general and phonics in particular. Unfortunately, teachers and parents also often blame children, and too many students come to believe that their inability to spell is a sign that they are stupid. Wrong! Research shows there are other reasons for the perceived proliferation of misspellings. These reasons often have more to do with the richness and variety of children's written vocabulary today than with a general decline in spelling ability and instruction. This may also have more to do with the shift from reading to television, videos, and computer games as common leisure activities.

> When the spelling of a word affects meaning, as in the words *sulfite* and *sulfate* in science study, spelling does count. Students should know this and know why it counts.

Nonetheless, even poor spellers can improve, and should be encouraged to do so for the real purpose good spelling serves—being able to better communicate to the reader. Teachers who use this book will find many ways to help all children become better spellers.

HOW IS THIS BOOK DIFFERENT FROM OTHER SPELLING PROGRAMS?

In this book, we outline a program that focuses on understanding
- the process of spelling
- the reasons for certain spellings when there is little relationship to the way a word is pronounced
- the relationship between spelling and meaning
- strategies that can be used in solving spelling problems
- when conventional spelling really does matter, when it doesn't matter, and how to know the difference

Traditional spelling programs generally follow a routine whereby children copy twenty unrelated words out of a text each Monday, complete exercises, memorize the words, then take a test on Friday.

This program doesn't work that way. The following chapters do not contain preselected, grade-leveled weekly word lists. They contain descriptions of activities designed to help children develop an understanding of words. Children then use that understanding to help them become proficient spellers. The Wordsmithing program has a Monday-to-Friday structure, with each day offering a selection of at least five activities based on word lists that you and your students have chosen. Most of the activities can be conducted with any set of words and at any grade level after children have begun to read and write independently. We have also left room for you to add other effective spelling ideas you have collected or developed over the years.

KEY POINTS FOR WORDSMITHING

1. Playing with words is key to learning about and becoming comfortable with them.
2. Understanding why words are spelled as they are gives students control of the spelling process.
3. Talking about words and strategies for spelling helps poor spellers grow in their understanding of what good spellers do. It makes the invisible (thought processes) visible to the learner.
4. Wordsmithing involves play, talk, understanding, creation, and control over words.

OVERVIEW OF THE PROGRAM

Monday	Collecting the Words (20 minutes)
Tuesday	Taking a Closer Look (10-20 minutes)
Wednesday	Making Sense of Words (10-20 minutes)
Thursday	Playing with Words (20 minutes)
Friday	Showing What We Know (20-30 minutes)

1. **Monday: Collecting the Words.** On Monday, the class creates a word collection based on a unifying theme or principle. Students select words from this list to make their personal word lists.
2. **Tuesday: Taking a Closer Look.** On Tuesday, students work on activities that focus on how letter-sound sequences impact on word spelling.
3. **Wednesday: Making Sense of Words.** On Wednesday, students work on activities that focus on developing generalities and recognizing patterns related to word meanings and origins.

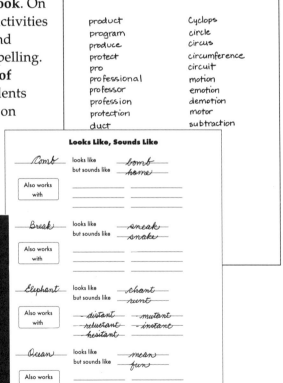

Introduction 5

4. **Thursday: Playing With Words.** On Thursday, students create and play word games.
5. **Friday: Showing What We Know.** On Friday, students do a spelling test or other activity to demonstrate what they have learned about their weekly word list.

Clues:
8. Can be a noun or an adverb.
7. Has 2 little words in it.
6. The little words each have 3 letters.
5. Its origin is Old English.
4. One part means "past".
3. The other part is in lots of words on the calendar.
2. It is near the end of the dictionary.
1. It means the day before today — the day that is already past.

SUMMARY

In this book we share many ideas that have worked for us, and others that we have gathered from colleagues. We invite you to try those strategies that fit your students' needs, your classroom organization, and your own teaching style.

When using this program, remember that word play is key to learning about words. Understanding why words are spelled as they are and talking about words and strategies for spelling help poor spellers understand what good spellers do.

Monday: Collecting the Words

Monday activities are designed to help teachers and children generate a set of words for the class to study during the rest of the week. Each collection of words has a unifying theme based on relationships of meaning or on spelling patterns. Unifying themes or principles can be found in other curricular units, through misspellings identified in children's writing, and through identification of common spelling patterns. Because students are involved in the generation of word lists, they may contain words they are using in their written work, words related to concepts they are studying in other subjects, words that contain difficult spelling patterns, or simply those that are intriguing.

From the large collection of words generated by the class, students select either a class word list or their own personal word lists for the week. While class word lists are the same for every student in the class, personal lists will vary in length and difficulty depending on an individual student's ability and needs. You may want to start the program by having students select a class word list from the larger class collection of words. As you and your students gain familiarity with this process, try personal word lists. Personal word lists, selected from the large class collection of words, allow for individual differences in ability while keeping the class as a whole focused on a particular spelling pattern, theme, principle, or strategy.

Both class and personal word lists consist entirely of words selected from the class collection of words generated on Mondays. This ensures that the principle or theme of the week is common to all students, even when the personal word lists differ. This provides a unifying context for all word study.

> Be sure to analyze the spelling errors your students are producing in their written work to find the underlying principle or pattern they need to study. Don't just collect errors and list them, because then you are back to a spelling approach based on memorizing rather than understanding.

KEY POINTS FOR MONDAY

➤ Students are involved in the development of the class list (ownership).
➤ They should generate this list from themes, topics, subject areas, or events that are already taking place in the classroom (relevance).
➤ From the class word list, students select their own personal word list, choosing words that fit with their abilities, their interests, and their needs (choice).

Step by step

1. Identify the theme or principle—the "glue"—that makes this week's word list a collection or set.
2. Give two or three examples to students.
3. The class generates additional words for the collection or set.
4. Students continue collecting words individually or in small groups using one of the ideas found in this chapter.

Note: In the samples shown on these two pages, the class and teacher could have created a class list of words selected from the class word collection. In Ms. Johnson's grade-five class, however, there is so much diversity of ability among the students that she always uses personal word lists.

Teacher's planning notes for sources of starter words

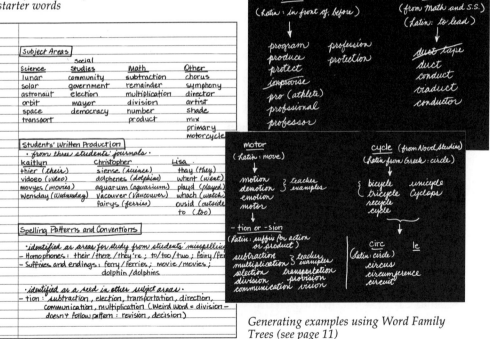

Generating examples using Word Family Trees (see page 11)

8 Building Connections: WORDSMITHING

5. The class pools their findings to create this week's class collection of words. The collection is recorded on chart paper and displayed.
6. Students select words from the class collection for either a class word list or for personal word lists for the week. They copy these into their notebooks using the contract format.
7. Teacher reviews students' word lists for correct spelling, then signs their spelling contract forms.
8. Students share lists with parents, and parents sign contract form.
9. Students are ready for Tuesday's spelling activities.

Class word collection

product, program, produce, protect, pro, professional, professor, profession, protection, duct, conduct, viaduct, conductor, motorcycle, bicycle, tricycle, unicycle, cycle

Cyclops, circle, circus, circumference, circuit, motion, emotion, demotion, motor, subtraction, multiplication, division, vision, provision, selection, communication, transportation

Spelling contract

Spelling Contract

Name: Carolyn
Week of: October 7–11

I have agreed to study the following __16__ words from this week's Class Word Collection.

1. geometry
2. geology
3. geography
4. geode
5. geometric
6. geographic
7. metric
8. metre
9. geological
10. centimetre
11. kilometre
12. millimetre
13. cent
14. century
15. centurion
16. centipede

My spelling partner for this week is Susan

Student Signature: Carolyn
Partner Signature: Susan
Teacher Signature: A. Smith
Parent(s) Signature(s): Anna Jones, Hal Jones

Notes: I only took 16 words this week because they were all pretty hard words. —C.J.

Kaitlyn
October 7 to 11

I have agreed to study the following 20 words from this week's Class Word Collection.

1. professional
2. professor
3. protection
4. viaduct
5. conductor
6. emotion
7. unicycle
8. product
9. motorcycle
10. recycle
11. Cyclops
12. circus
13. circuit
14. circumference
15. multiplication
16. provision
17. transportation
18. circle
19. communication
20. selection

My Spelling partner for this week is Jorge

Kaitlyn
Jorge
A. Smith
Mrs. Mendoza

Personal word list

Monday: Collecting the Words 9

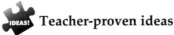 **Teacher-proven ideas**

Some of the ways you can work with your students to generate lists are

    Spelling Spines **10**
    Word Family Trees **11**
    The Secret of Nyms **13**
    Contractions, Compounds, and Conundrums **14**
    Quick Fixes **15**
    Sounds Like/Looks Like **16**
    Enviroprint **18**

❋ Monday: SPELLING SPINES

Spelling Spines provide a way to organize word families based on spelling patterns such as *a-u* (*aunt, taut, taught, author, caught, cauterize, naughty*). This activity helps familiarize children with common letter sequences, and in some cases, the rationale behind their use. There are a number of common, recurring spelling patterns in English. Some, such as *a-n*—found in words such as *ran, fan, man, and, stand, banner*—simply share a sequence of letters. Other groups of words that share a letter sequence have additional commonalities. For example, the *i-g-h* words are carry-overs from the Old English spellings. The pronunciations of *sigh, night, neigh, neighbor, weigh, fight,* and so on have changed over time, but the spellings haven't. Some common spelling patterns yield different sounds (e.g. *height* and *weight, eat* and *great*). This is an opportunity to point out and discuss some of these idiosyncracies.

Step by step

1. Select a common spelling pattern based on the needs of students in your class.
2. Use a Spelling Spine format on the board. For five minutes, fill in as many "ribs" as possible on the spine.
3. Students select words from the class collection generated on the spine to create their personal word lists for

the week. They copy these into their notebooks using the contract format.
4. Teacher reviews students' personal word lists for appropriate level of difficulty and correct spelling, then signs their spelling contract forms.
5. Students share list with parents, and parents sign contract form.
6. Students are ready for Tuesday's spelling activities.

Spelling Spines

❋ Monday: WORD FAMILY TREES

Word Family Trees are word families based on meaning. For example, the word *transport* is a marriage of *trans* (change/across) and *port* (carry). *Trans* has the relatives *translate, transfer, transmission*—all of which have something to do with moving or changing. *Port* has the relatives *portable, import, porter*—all of which have something to do with carrying. This strategy is used to generate a class list that demonstrates the relationship between meaning and spelling. This is one way to unlock the spelling structure when phonetic strategies don't work. It is useful for helping students understand word meanings and origins. This strategy works with compound words and words that consist of two or more roots, prefixes, or suffixes.

Step by step

1. Select words from social studies, science, language arts; or select words that capture the interest of your class. In a dictionary that gives word origins, look up the words and word parts.
2. To demonstrate, draw the Word Family Tree format (see example) on the board with your chosen word example. With the class, generate a few related words as an example.
3. Have students add to the lists using their own Word Family Trees.
4. Students report the words they've listed on their Word Family Trees.
5. The class pools their findings to create this week's class collection of words. The collection is recorded on chart paper and displayed.
6. Students select words from the class collection for their personal word lists for the week. They copy these into their notebooks using the contract format.
7. Teacher reviews students' personal word lists for appropriate level of difficulty and correct spelling, then signs their spelling contract forms.
8. Students share list with parents, and parents sign contract form.
9. Students are ready for Tuesday's spelling activities.

Encourage students to use members of their new word family in their journals, assignments, and any other writing activities, and to watch and listen for these words in books, the news, and other day-to-day language.

Word Family Tree		Word Family Tree *television*	
		tele	**vision**
		Origin: Greek; tele = far off	Origin: Latin; vis = see (vid)
		telephone	video
		telegraph	visit
		telegram	invisible
		teleport	visitor
			visible
			vision
			vista
			Visine (eye drops)
			visitor

Blank format; Word Family Tree for word television

❋ Monday: THE SECRET OF NYMS

Homonyms, antonyms, and synonyms—once children begin to learn about words, they'll know that *homo* means *same*, *anti* means *opposite* or *against*, and *syn* means *alike*. The problem of keeping these terms clear is solved! Keeping homonyms sorted out isn't always easy, so collecting and focusing on them for a week can certainly help. While antonyms and synonyms may not pose any particular spelling problems they can be used as the basis for interesting word collections.[1]

Step by step

1. Select the type—homonyms, antonyms or synonyms.
2. Provide a definition and an example.
3. In small groups, students think of and record in ten minutes as many additional examples as they can.
4. Students report their findings.
5. The class pools their findings to create this week's class collection of words. The collection is recorded on chart paper and displayed.
6. Students select words from the class collection to create their personal word lists for the week. They copy these into their notebooks using the contract format.
7. Teacher reviews students' personal word lists for the appropriate level of difficulty and correct spelling, then signs their spelling contract forms.
8. Students share lists with parents, and parents sign contract form.
9. Students are ready for Tuesday's spelling activities.

Secret of Nyms

---

1. Homonyms are broken into two types in some reference and text books: homographs, which are words that are written the same but sound different or mean different things, and homophones, which are words that sound the same but are written differently.

❋ Monday: Contractions, Compounds, and Conundrums

Conundrums are riddles or hard puzzles. For some children, contractions and compound words can be puzzling. Others are confused by abbreviations, acronyms (including those like *ROM* which have come to be used as words), and purposeful misspellings (such as *lite, krazy,* and others used in advertising). Exploring the origins and uses of these types of words can help lead to better spelling.

Step by step

1. Based on your students' needs, select a particular word type (contractions, compound words, abbreviations, acronyms, advertisement spellings).
2. Introduce and explain the type; then provide a couple of examples.
3. Students build the collection by having a word hunt, highlighting appropriate words in magazines and newspapers.
4. Students report their findings.
5. The class pools their findings to create this week's class collection of words. The collection is recorded on chart paper and displayed.
6. Students select words from the class collection to create their personal word lists for the week. They copy these into their notebooks using the contract format.
7. Teacher reviews students' personal word lists for appropriate level of difficulty and correct spelling, then signs their spelling contract forms.

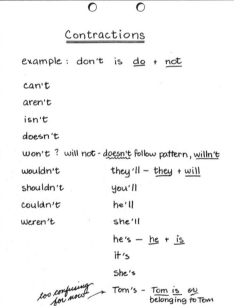

Class list of contractions

8. Students share lists with parents, and parents sign contract form.
9. Students are ready for Tuesday's spelling activities.

❋ Monday: QUICK FIXES—PREFIXES AND SUFFIXES

Knowing about prefixes and suffixes can help children unlock both the meanings and spellings of words. The only reliable rule for adding suffixes is "Change the *y* to *i* before adding *ed*." Beyond that, there are so many exceptions that it is more effective for most children (and adults, too) to look for spelling patterns rather than trying to memorize a number of not-always-valid rules.

Step by step

1. Introduce two or more prefixes or suffixes that have the same effect on words, for example *non-*, *un-*, and *dis-* (which make a word into its opposite) or *-er* and *-tion* (which can make verbs into nouns).
2. Use clues to help students understand how the prefix or suffix affects the meaning of the root words. For example, you can give the clues, "If your shoe is not tied then it is _____", and "If you are not happy, you are _____." Stress that you want the same word (*tied, happy*) with a new part added to it (*untied, unhappy*). Students determine through examples and discussions that *un-* means *not*.
3. Have students generate words that use the identified prefixes or suffixes, using dictionaries, thesauri, and any other classroom resources. Have students underline the most basic root word.
4. Students report their findings.
5. The class pools their findings to create this week's class collection of words. The collection is recorded on chart paper and displayed.
6. Students select words from the class collection to create their personal word lists for the week. They copy these into their notebooks using the contract format.

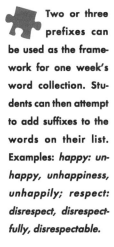 Two or three prefixes can be used as the framework for one week's word collection. Students can then attempt to add suffixes to the words on their list. Examples: *happy: unhappy, unhappiness, unhappily; respect: disrespect, disrespectfully, disrespectable.*

7. Teacher reviews students' personal word lists for appropriate level of difficulty and correct spelling, then signs their spelling contract forms.
8. Students share lists with parents, and parents sign contract form.
9. Students are ready for Tuesday's spelling activities.

Selections for This Week's Collection

agreement *   happier *   * from last week
appointment * healthier *
apartment   steadier *   Note: Be prepared to add prefixes non, un, dis to these words. Also be prepared for -iest and -ily endings!
department   funnier
compartment   sillier

Word Quilting Bee this Friday.

Quick Fixes

Last Week	This Week	
	Brainstorm	
disagree	disagreement	disagreeable
	agreement	agreeable
unhappy	happiness	happier
	happily	happiest
unhealthy	healthiness	healthier
	healthily	healthiest
unsteady	steadier	steadiness
	steadiest	steadily
disappoint	appointment	appointed
nonsense	sensible	sensitive
	sensor	sensation
nonstop	stopper	stoppable
	stoppage	unstoppable
unknown	known (has a suffix!)	
	knowable	knowledge
disturb	turb ??	disturber
	disturbance	
unkempt	kempt ??	kept ?? keep ??

❈ Monday: Sounds Like/Looks Like

This activity is designed to help children formulate generalizations about common spelling patterns and to develop lists of words that do and don't fit the pattern. Although we learned many of these generalizations as "rules," we have since discovered that many of these rules are wrong more often than they are right.

Step by step

1. Select a spelling pattern (e.g.; *tion*) or question (e.g., "When does *c* represent the *s* sound and when does it represent the *k* sound?").
2. Brainstorm some words that fit the pattern.

3. Have small groups of students add to the list and develop tentative generalizations. Encourage use of personal and class dictionaries.
4. Groups share their generalizations and reasoning with the class.
5. Brainstorm exceptions—words that don't follow the pattern.
6. Test the generalization to see when it doesn't work. Make a list of all the words found for which this generalization doesn't work. Try to find another generalization that will work with this new set of words.
7. Record the class decision regarding the generalization.
8. Have the class pool their findings to create this week's class collection of words. The collection is recorded on chart paper and displayed.
9. Students select words from the class collection to create their personal word lists for the week. They copy these into their notebooks using the contract format.
10. Teacher reviews students' personal word lists for appropriate level of difficulty and correct spelling, then signs their spelling contract forms.
11. Students share lists with parents, and parents sign contract form.
12. Students are ready for Tuesday's spelling activities.

When c sounds like k
it looks like cr

ic	co
ac	ca
oc	cl
ec	

Examples: cream cork catch clock
frantic action occupy electric

When c sounds like s
it looks like

| ce | ci | ence | ance |
| cy | | | |

Examples: dance city science attendance France century fancy

Sounds Like/Looks Like

❋ Monday: ENVIROPRINT

Words abound in our environment at school, at home, in the community, and even in the "virtual" environment of the Internet. Although these words don't usually work well for exploring spelling patterns or word families, they can be used to generate related words, to practice adding prefixes and suffixes, or to investigate word origins.

> For homework, have students compile home enviroprint lists. One teacher prohibited the opening of cupboards while compiling the list. She wanted her students to focus on the print that is always visible in the house, not on food tin labels.

Step by step

1. Introduce the activity by beginning a discussion about words in the environment, such as those found on signs, graffiti, and in advertisements.
2. Take the class for a walk around the school or neighborhood to collect words. Some teachers send their students out with instant cameras or clipboards.
3. Students report words they found in the environment.
4. The class pools their findings to create this week's class collection of words. The collection is recorded on chart paper and displayed.
5. Students select words from the class collection to create their personal word lists for the week. They copy these into their notebooks using the contract format.
6. Teacher reviews students' personal word lists for appropriate level of difficulty and correct spelling, then signs their spelling contract forms.

Enviroprint

7. Students share list with parents, and parents sign contract form.
8. Students are ready for Tuesday's spelling activities.

SUMMARY

For Monday activities, remember to involve students in the development of the class list. They should generate words that are relevant to themes, topics, subjects, or events in the classroom. From the class word list, students select personal word lists that fit with their abilities, their interests, and their needs.

Monday: Personal Favorites, New and Old

MONDAY: PERSONAL FAVORITES, NEW AND OLD

MONDAY: PERSONAL FAVORITES, NEW AND OLD

TUESDAY: TAKING A CLOSER LOOK

Tuesday activities are designed so students stop and take a closer look at the words generated for the Monday word collection. Rather than focusing on meaning, Tuesday activities focus on the sounds and structure of words (the phonetics and the orthography). This helps students recognize patterns and develop generalizations they can apply to other words.

KEY POINTS FOR TUESDAY

- Students develop their own rules and generalizations rather than memorizing rules that often don't apply.
- There are patterns in spelling that can help us understand why words are spelled in certain ways.
- Discussion of why words are spelled in given ways is critical. Students need to understand conventions for adding endings and the effect these endings have on meaning. When students understand that *jumped* is *jump* that happened yesterday, they are less likely to spell it *jumpt*.

Step by step

1. Introduce the activity to the whole class. Provide examples and practice.
2. Give students time for independent practice.
3. Students record their learning in their spelling notebook.

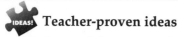 **Teacher-proven ideas**

Some of the ways to help your students take a closer look at words are

    Beginning, Ending, Middle **24**
    Word Parts **26**
    Happy Endings **27**
    Mistakes and Misdemeanors **29**
    Highlights **30**

❋ Tuesday: BEGINNING, ENDING, MIDDLE

Some students have difficulty sequencing the sounds and letters in words. Still others find it difficult to approach spelling using larger, letter-sound chunks, such as consonant blends, *r*-controlled vowels, and digraphs (*th, sh, ch, wh*). Sound and letter sequencing is one of those skills we often assume children just possess, but when their spelling patterns show confusion, as in *form* for *from*, *gril* for *girl*, and *was* for *saw*, it is often an indication that they don't have this skill.[1]

Step by step

1. Select one-syllable words from this week's class collection or pull one syllable from a larger word.
2. On the board, draw three horizontal lines, left to right: _____ _____ _____ .
3. Say the word or syllable, then record the first sound.
4. Say the word or syllable again and record the last sound.
5. Say the word or syllable again and fill in the middle.
6. Write the word or syllable beginning to end as you say the word out loud, emphasizing the sequence of sounds.
7. Choose another word.
8. Ask students to draw three lines on their papers, as above.
9. Dictate the word or syllable.

---

1. The McCracken spelling program *Spelling Through Phonics* is invaluable here.

10. Have students repeat the word, then say only the first sound. Then they write the letter or letters for that sound on the first line.
11. Read the word again. Students say and write the last sound on the last line.
12. Read the word again. Students say and fill in the middle.
13. Discuss the spellings produced, and add any additional letters. For example, the word *flake* could appear as *flak*. Discuss the need for something to "make the *a* say *a*" and add the final *e*.
14. Students say and write the whole word beginning to end.
15. Instruct students to look at the word or syllable closely, get a picture of it in their minds, cover it up, and write it again.
16. Students choose five words or syllables from this week's personal word list and find a partner to dictate the words or syllables to them. As the partner dictates, the student applies the beginning, ending, middle strategy as practiced earlier.
17. Students record this work in their spelling notebooks.

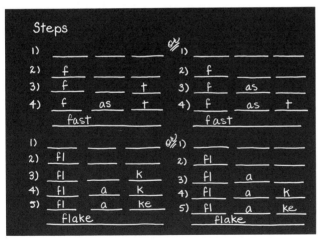

Beginning, Middle, End

❈ Tuesday: WORD PARTS

Some students can manage the sequencing aspect of spelling with words of one or two syllables but get lost with longer words. Although they might be able to spell *in, for, ma,* and *tion,* the word *information* as a whole overwhelms them. These students often benefit from learning how to break words into more manageable parts. Avoid formal syllabification rules at this point, and focus instead on natural breaks in words. Point out how the parts are spelled if they appear inside a word rather than as stand-alone words. For example, *ma* in *information* is inside a word, so it doesn't need the *y* that the stand-alone word *may* would need.

Step by step

1. Select a word from this week's word collection (begin with phonetically regular two-syllable words).
2. Say the word, slightly emphasizing the syllables.
3. Ask students to say the word with you.
4. Say it again, tapping out the syllables. Ask: "How many parts?"
5. Say to the students, "Say only the first part with me. After I say the first part you say the second part." Play with this. Say first part, then they say next part. Or they say the first part and you say the next part.
6. Divide the class and take turns saying parts in and out of order.
7. Ask students to pick five words from their personal word list that might cause them difficulty.
8. Working with a partner, students take turns saying word parts.

pumpkin	sunset	relatives
dragon	benefit	criminal
mother	Saturday	establish
summer	suddenly	television
around	another	motorcycle
before	Canada	information
morning	elephant	transportation
something	afternoon	particular
thirteen	hospital	responsible
fourteen	tomorrow	superstition
fifteen	wonderful	undercover
twenty	eleven	helicopter
hundred	computer	advertisement
almost	yesterday	universal
behind	reminder	supersonic
birthday	remember	invitation
myself	adventure	communicate
candy	important	discover
Sunday	completely	computer
combat		

Two-, three-, and four-syllable words

9. After lots of oral word-part practice, students are ready to write the word parts.
10. Ask students to say and tap the word parts, draw that many lines in their notebook, and fill them in appropriately. For example:
    ‣ after = af / ter = two parts
    ‣ Draw two lines: _____ _____.
    ‣ Say and write the first part: _af_ .
    ‣ Say and write the next part: _ter_ .
11. Students write the word, beginning to end, in one piece, while they say it. This part of the exercise is very important. It helps embed the sight, sound, and feel of the word in the students' minds.
12. Students look at the word closely, get a picture of it in their minds, cover it, and write it again.

Student sample

🌸 Tuesday: HAPPY ENDINGS

Adding common endings to words—for example, *s, es, ed, ing,* and *er*—can cause spelling mistakes. This activity is designed to help children understand the role of these common endings and to expand the uses of the words on their personal word lists. For example, from the word *walk*, they would learn *walks, walking, walker,* and *walked*. For older students, this list of common endings can be extended to plurals, possessives, and plural possessives, such as *elephants, elephant's,* and *elephants'*.

Tuesday: Taking a Closer Look

Discussion questions for adding endings: Which of the words in this week's collection can be made plural? Why can't the other words be made plural? What happens to some of these words if we add an *s*? What do the words that can be made plural have in common? (All nouns.) The words that can't be made plural? (All verbs.) Can you think of any words that are made plural in some way other than by adding *s*?

Step by step

1. On the board, write the endings to be used this week.
2. Choose three words from this week's word collection.
3. Add endings, discussing the effect each has on the word. For example, "Adding *e-d* changes a verb to its past tense. Past tense means that we're talking about something that has already happened."
4. Look for patterns—consonant doubling, changing *y* to *i*, dropping the final *e*.
5. Formulate generalizations by asking a question such as, "Can we find any patterns when adding endings to words that end in the letter *s*?"
6. Students choose six different words from their personal word lists. In their notebooks, they list these words and, where appropriate, add the endings.

	Jonah
leaf	leaf – leaves, leafing, leafed
stream	
beach	
each	
breathe	breathe – breathing, breathless
team	
search	
sneak	
reach	reach – reaches, reaching, reached
real	
earth	earth –
dream	
beam	
peach	pe
reality	re
steal	

Happy Endings exercise

Instructions: Pick any 6 words from your personal word list and add s, es, ed, or ing. Only add an ending if it works. Remember: don't pick "each" — none of the endings work.

✸ Tuesday: MISTAKES AND MISDEMEANORS

Many English words can be "legally" spelled a number of ways—that is, by using a common or recognized spelling pattern. From observing words, students can determine common spelling patterns and rules. For example, *gh* can represent the *f* sound, but never at the beginning of the word. By exploring the various spellings that could be used to represent a given word, children become familiar with English spelling patterns. This activity teaches children a strategy for trying out a number of spellings when their first try doesn't look right, and for finding words in the dictionary.

Step by step

1. As a teaching example, select a common one-syllable word such as *leaf, bright,* or *take,* preferably from the class word collection.
2. Brainstorm as many spellings as possible.
3. Discuss each spelling given using the following questions:
   - Is it "legal"? (Does it follow an established spelling pattern?)
   - What makes it legal?
   - Are there other words with this spelling pattern?
   - What do we know about this word that might explain its spelling pattern?
   - Are there any mnemonic devices (memory tricks) that might help with remembering the correct spelling?
4. Ask students to pick one word with a partner and generate as many creative spellings as possible. Have them record these in their notebooks and identify which spellings are legal. These can be shared with the class or with parents.

Mistakes and Misdemeanors

❋ Tuesday: HIGHLIGHTS

For some students, highlighting silent letters, difficult letter sequences, small words within words, or other interesting aspects of a word can be an effective word-memory strategy. Highlighting visually interesting letter patterns such as the *e-v-e* in the word *reverse*, the double *l*'s in *parallel*, or the two *o*'s in *doctor* or *rotor* (which is spelled the same backwards or forwards) can help students retain a visual image of the parts of the word they may be unsure of.

Step by step

1. Select a word from the class collection.
2. Discuss any visually interesting aspects of the spelling of the word.
3. Write the word on the board, using different colored chalk or markers for the highlighted parts.
4. Ask two student volunteers to choose two additional words and write them on the board. Have students explain why they highlighted the parts they did and how this will help them remember the word.
5. Students write words from personal word lists in their spelling notebooks and highlight interesting parts. Highlighting can be done with a highlighting pen or by using different colored pencils or pens.

Highlights

SUMMARY

For Tuesday activities, it's important that students develop their own rules and generalizations rather than memorizing rules that often don't apply. Students learn that there are patterns in spelling that can help us understand why words are spelled in certain ways. They also learn the conventions for adding endings and the effect these endings have on meaning.

TUESDAY: PERSONAL FAVORITES, NEW AND OLD

TUESDAY: PERSONAL FAVORITES, NEW AND OLD

WEDNESDAY: MAKING SENSE OF WORDS

On Wednesday, students make sense of words. They do this by comparing words, studying word origins, creating new words, and learning ways of remembering correct spellings. Wednesday activities help students connect words on their word list with knowledge they already have, and with new knowledge that helps them understand and remember how words are spelled.

KEY POINTS FOR WEDNESDAY

- There are fun things that we can do to help us remember how things are spelled.
- Children learn to think about how words are connected to their experience.
- Knowing about the origins and meanings of words helps students understand the relationship between meaning and spelling, as well as the relationship among different words.

Step by step

1. Introduce the activity to the whole class. Provide examples and practice.
2. Give students time for independent practice.
3. Students record their learning in their spelling notebook.

Teacher-proven ideas

Some of the ways teachers have found effective to help students make sense of words are

> Noisy Mnemonics 34
> Looks Like/Sounds Like 35
> Word Origins 36
> Thesaurus Rex 37
> Clues 38
> Inventions 39

❋ Wednesday: NOISY MNEMONICS

Mnemonic (*ni-mon-ik*) devices are systems for remembering. For example, one way to remember how to spell *mnemonic* is to say to yourself, "*Mnemonic* has to do with memory, so it starts with an *m*." Most people use mnemonic devices without realizing it. When we chant "*M-i*-double-*s-i*-double-*s-i*-double-*p-i*" (*Mississippi*), or "at-ten-dance" (*attendance*), or "the principal is my pal" (*principal*), we are using mnemonics. We can also create word pictures. For example, thinking of the single *m* in *camel* as a double hump helps us remember not to double the *m*, or the camel would have a very funny-looking hump. Children often enjoy learning and creating oral and visual mnemonic devices, and for some, it is an effective way to remember particularly tricky spellings.

> Create posters of mnemonic devices for a spelling display or class bulletin board. Collecting mnemonics from parents and other adults makes an interesting homework assignment.

Step by step

1. Share a number of mnemonic devices, such as those given above, in the sample at right, or others you may know.
2. Invite children to create and share mnemonic devices for words from this week's word collection.

Mnemonics

3. Provide opportunities for students to share their mnemonic devices orally.
4. In their notebooks, have students record two or three mnemonic devices for words from their personal word list.

✤ Wednesday: LOOKS LIKE/SOUNDS LIKE

This chanting activity involves a form of mnemonic device. It helps children connect common words that have phonetically irregular spellings to known words. Be sure to choose phonetically regular words for the looks-like and sounds-like parts.

Step by step

1. As a teaching example, choose a high-frequency, nonphonetic word, such as *come*.
2. Find a word that sounds different but looks similar, such as *home*.
3. Create a chant by finding a word that sounds like *come* but is phonetically regular, such as *gum*:

    Come looks like *home* but sounds like *gum*.
    Said looks like *raid* but sounds like *red*.

4. Students create chants from words on their personal word lists, then record these in their notebooks.
5. As a class, students create additional chants. Have students create posters for the classroom from these. Add a list of any other words that follow the pattern of the three words in the chant.

Looks Like, Sounds Like

❉ Wednesday: WORD ORIGINS

Students need access to dictionaries and reference books that contain information on word origins. Knowing where words come from sometimes helps students understand why they are spelled as they are. This understanding can help them remember the spelling pattern.

Step by step

1. Students select a word from their personal word lists and find out everything they can about their words.
2. This information is recorded in their notebooks. It can be shared with the class.
3. Information can be shared with the class in a number of ways:
   - Students create posters, diagrams, or act out a pantomime.
   - Words from the class collection can be drawn from a hat or given by the teacher, secretly. Students find word information and, on Thursday, use it in a game of Trivia or twenty questions.
   - Small groups of students can select six or eight words, research them, and use the information to create clues and crosswords (see pages 38, 49).
   - Students can create a dictionary of a particular family of words. One class created an illustrated dictionary of -ology words, and learned a lot about prefixes such as bio-, theo-, paleo-, and geo- in the process.

Word Origins

My Word is Biology

Bio means: to do with life or living things
It is from the Greek word bios.
logy means: subject of study
It is a suffix.
It turns words into nouns.
It is from the Greek word logos or logia (Greek suffix)

Biology is a science about living things — plants and animals. People who study biology are called biologists. We study biology in science class when we learn about plants, animals and the human body.

Other bio words are:
biography biochemistry antibiotic

❋ Wednesday: THESAURUS REX

Students become familiar with the thesaurus as they explore words in their personal word collections. Many professional writers use a thesaurus to add variety, precision, and elegance to their writing. Children discover that even words considered to be synonyms have nuances or shades of meaning that make them different. For example, the thesaurus listings for *walk* include *amble, stroll, stride,* and *pace.* Thesauri are available in junior versions, but adult editions are much richer. Children need to have access to both.

Build a class thesaurus by putting Thesaurus Rex sheets in a binder. A new Thesaurus Rex sheet is added as more meanings are found.

Step by step

1. Select a word from the class collection. Show students how to use the thesaurus to find the word and its synonyms. It helps to display the relevant page from the thesaurus on an overhead transparency.
2. Students select a word from their personal word lists and look it up in the thesaurus. They then choose three of the synonyms given, look them up in the dictionary, and record them in their notebooks.

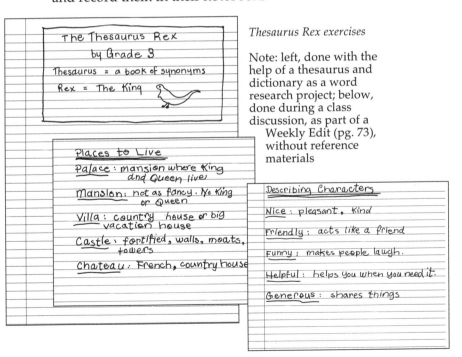

Thesaurus Rex exercises

Note: left, done with the help of a thesaurus and dictionary as a word research project; below, done during a class discussion, as part of a Weekly Edit (pg. 73), without reference materials

Wednesday: Making Sense of Words   37

❋ Wednesday: CLUES

Children develop clues about certain words from the class word collection. In addition to using definitions of the words as clues, they use information such as the word origin, a spelling pattern that occurs in the word, or information on the word's meaning family. This activity requires lots of modeling and support at first.

Students can create crossword puzzles, word searches (using clues instead of words), matching games, or Trivia questions. These activities could then be used in centers, at home with parents or siblings, or in class on Thursday.

Step by step

1. Select two or three words from the class collection to demonstrate how clues are created. Create the clues with students. Record on the blackboard.
2. Ask students to choose their own word from the class list and create clues about it. Have them report back to the class.
3. Students are asked to select other words from the classroom word collection and develop clues about them. Clues are based on origins, spelling patterns, how the word changes when adding a suffix, derivations, and other word-family members. These are the kinds of clues that encourage children to think about words and their structures.
4. Each student's clues are recorded in their notebooks. They can later be used to create games (see Thursday: Class Puzzles, page 49).

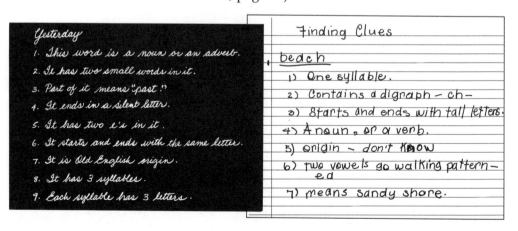

❦ Wednesday: INVENTIONS

Children make sense of words by taking parts of words having specific meaning and combining them to create new words.

Step by step

1. Share examples of recently created words, such as *microwave, astronaut,* and *cyberspace,* and discuss how they got their names. Use the dictionary to find roots if necessary.
2. Have each student create a new, unique word by combining parts of words from their personal word list. Students then write a definition for the new word that reflects the meanings of the word parts selected. They may add affixes, words, or word parts from sources other than the word list, as long as one part of their new word is from the list.
3. In their notebooks, students record their new words and definitions, then share them with the class.

Students represent the new word using a web, illustration, diagram, or descriptive paragraph. Students can create advertisements for the new product their word describes, such as, "The Aquanaut Jet Ski."

Where did these words come from?

microwave: micro = small (Greek)
wave = motion (?) (Old English)
An oven that uses short electromagnetic waves is called a microwave oven.

television: tele = far off (Greek)
vision = see (Latin)
We can see things from far away on a television.

astronaut: astro = star (Greek)
naut = sailor (Greek)
An astronaut travels on a space ship.

hydroelectricity: hydro = water (Greek)
electricity = amber (??) (Greek)
Hydroelectricity is electricity from a dam. The water going through the dam makes electricity.

minivan: mini = least (Latin, minim)
mini means small nowadays
van = abbreviation for caravan
caravan = trailer home (French) or large vehicle
Minivan means a small, large vehicle.
(What! This doesn't make sense.)

My Words, My Inventions

1) microcomp: micro = small (Greek)
comp = short for computer
A microcomp is a small computer that fits on your arm like a watch.

2) aquanaut: aqua = water (Latin)
naut = sailor (Greek)
An aquanaut is a sort of jet ski that people can ride across the lake on.

3) astrovision: astro = star
vision = see
An astrovision is a telescope you can wear like glasses and see the stars like you could with a regular telescope.

Inventions

SUMMARY

On Wednesday, children learn about words by connecting them to their experience. They develop ways of remembering and learn about the origins and meanings of words. This helps them understand the relationship between meaning and spelling as well as the relationships among different words.

WEDNESDAY: PERSONAL FAVORITES, NEW AND OLD

WEDNESDAY: PERSONAL FAVORITES, NEW AND OLD

THURSDAY: PLAYING WITH WORDS

Play is a part of learning—and learning to play with words is a way of coming to understand how words work.

KEY POINTS FOR THURSDAY

- Word play is another way of encouraging students to explore words, word meanings, and spelling patterns.
- Word play is not only fun, it's educational. Brain research has shown that we learn more quickly when we are actively engaged in learning. Fun is engaging.
- Children often make up games. Encourage them to make up word games. These promote creativity and exploration, both of which enhance learning.

Step by step

1. Teach students how to play one of the games by playing it with the whole class.
2. The class generates the instructions for the game in their own words. Record and post the instructions for the game.
3. The following week, students play the game in pairs or small groups, using the current week's word collection.
4. Once the students know a few games, they may choose the games they want to play to practice words from their word lists.

Teacher-proven ideas

Teachers have found the following games to be useful with a wide variety of word collections.

> Twenty Word Questions 44
> The Dictionary Game 46
> Spelling-Clue Countdown 47
> Mystery Pictures 48
> Class Puzzles 49
> Game Over 50
> Commercially Produced Word Games 51

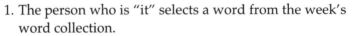 **Thursday: TWENTY WORD QUESTIONS**

Twenty Word Questions is played just like Twenty Questions except, instead of selecting an object or person, a person designated as "it" selects a word from this week's class collection. The object of the game is for the players to identify the word before they use up all twenty questions.

Step by step

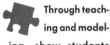 Through teaching and modeling, show students how to ask questions related to word structure. Questions about syllables, consonants, vowels, and endings, for example, can quickly narrow down the choices.

1. The person who is "it" selects a word from the week's word collection.
2. Other students in the group take turns asking yes or no questions about the word.
3. "It" keeps track of the number of questions asked.
4. If no one identifies the selected word within twenty questions, the game is over and "it" chooses someone new to be "it". The new "it" selects a word and starts a new game.
5. If someone does identify the word before twenty questions are used up, that person is "it" and selects a new word.

Following is an example of what this game sounded like using the word *continent*, which was chosen from a grade-six class collection:

1. Is it a noun? *Yes*
2. Is it a proper noun? *No*
3. Can it be made plural? *Yes*
4. Does it have more than one syllable? *Yes*
5. Does it have two syllables? *No*
6. Does it have three syllables? *Yes*
7. Does it start with a vowel? *No*
8. Does it end with a vowel? *No*
9. Could you add *ing* to it? *No*
10. Is it a person? *No*
11. Is it a place? *Yes*
12. Does it have an *a* in it? *No*
13. Does it have an *i* in it? *Yes*
14. Does it have two *t*'s in it? *Yes*
15. Is it *continent*? *Yes!*

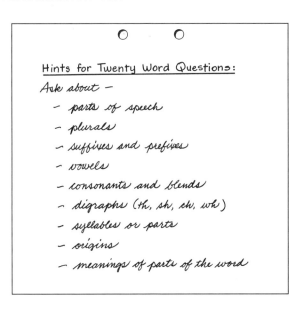

Hints for Twenty Word Questions:

Ask about —
- parts of speech
- plurals
- suffixes and prefixes
- vowels
- consonants and blends
- digraphs (th, sh, ch, wh)
- syllables or parts
- origins
- meanings of parts of the word

❋ Thursday: THE DICTIONARY GAME

This game involves using what we know about words while having fun. All you need is a class set of dictionaries and this week's class word collection.

Step by step

1. The teacher chooses a word from the class collection, looks it up in the dictionary, and reads only the definition. (Try to conceal the dictionary so that students won't get any extra clues about the location of the word in the dictionary. Or, you can look the word up ahead of time and record the definition and dictionary page number on a scrap of paper.)
2. With their dictionaries closed, students make "thought pictures" as you read the definition. Give them a few seconds to continue jotting down thoughts about the word before you say "Go," or "Open dictionary," or "Start."
3. Students look up the word they think matches the definition given.
4. If they find a match, they go to the board and write down the page number on which they found the word.
5. Other students turn to the correct page number and try to find the matching word.
6. After several students have found the word, instruct them to help someone else find it. Continue to help until everyone has found it.
7. Ask the original "finder" how he or she knew what the word was. Were there meaning clues? Word-part clues? Part-of-speech clues? What was on her "thought picture?" Encourage students to use all their knowledge about words and word parts when playing this game.

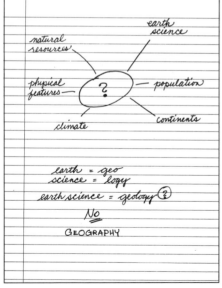

Dictionary Game thought picture for word geography

✸ Thursday: SPELLING-CLUE COUNTDOWN[1]

This game provides practice in thinking about word origins, meaning relationships, and spelling patterns.

Step by step

1. Students select a word from this week's personal word collection and create a set of five to ten clues about the word. Information on the origin of the word, the part of speech (i.e., noun, verb, adjective, etc.), its spelling pattern, related words or derivatives, synonyms or antonyms can all be included. Students can work individually, in pairs, or in small groups. If done individually, the information gathered during Wednesday's Word Clues or Word Origin activities can be used as a starting point for developing the clues.

2. The student or group of students order the clues from the most general—clue five—to the most specific—clue one.

3. Clues are presented and counted down one at a time, in general to specific order. The class or opposite team attempts to guess the word before all the clues are given.

4. The last clue, clue one, is usually a dead giveaway, because it provides specific information, such as the definition of the word or how many times a given letter appears in the word.

Spelling clues can also be used to create a word trivia game.

Clues:
8. Can be a noun or an adverb.
7. Has 2 little words in it.
6. The little words each have 3 letters.
5. Its origin is Old English.
4. One part means "past".
3. The other part is in lots of words on the calendar.
2. It is near the end of the dictionary.
1. It means the day before today — the day that is already past.

Spelling Clue Countdown for the word yesterday

---

1. Based on "Clue Countdowns" from the book *Literacy through Literature*. Thanks to Terry Johnson and Daphne Louis.

✽ Thursday: MYSTERY PICTURES

Some students are able to do and enjoy this activity, while others find it almost impossible to do. Pairing a student who is visually oriented with one who is good at word play can make this a successful activity for both.

Step by step

1. Student selects a word from the class collection.
2. Student creates an illustration that contains clues to the word selected. There are many types of clues, including sound-alikes, rebuses, and word-part clues.
3. Illustrations can be posted on a bulletin board so that other students can try to guess the word represented by the clues in the illustration.

> Word origins are found in most adult dictionaries. Have students search for clues about their mystery pictures.

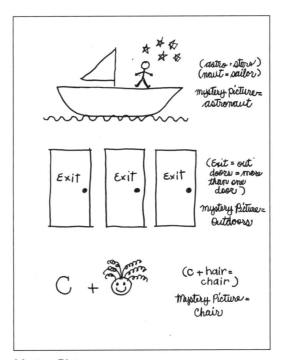

Mystery Pictures

❋ Thursday: CLASS PUZZLES

Many of the activities children do earlier in the week can be the basis for games or puzzles on Thursday. Some puzzles the students might create are crosswords, word searches, anagrams, or word scrambles. Computer programs for creating some of these games are available; students often enjoy using them. Be sure you get a program that allows the user to input their own words and clues. For those who don't use computers, graph paper is a must for creating crosswords and word searches. Students can trade their puzzles with each other for Thursday night homework.

Step by step

1. Demonstrate how to create a word search, crossword, or other puzzle, using graph paper or a computer program.
2. Students create puzzles using words from the class collection.
3. Puzzles can be traded between students or placed in a binder for later use.
4. Students can select a game from the binder, have it photocopied, and use it for homework, extra credit, or, when they have a few extra minutes during the day, for fun.
5. Word searches, crosswords, and other student-made puzzles from previous weeks can be used as review for the whole class or for individual students.

Word-search puzzle

Note: In the word-search puzzle illustrated on page 49, words in the first column are from the class word collection. The words in the other two columns are those that fill in the blanks after the collection words were put in. Encourage students to fill in the leftover blanks with as many additional words as possible, rather than just slotting in random letters. Creating word-search puzzles by hand rather than on the computer gives students greater opportunities to think about word structure.

❋ Thursday: GAME OVER

This game is like Hangman, except it uses the words *Game Over* instead of *Hangman*.

Step by step

1. This is a two-person game. One person is "it".
2. "It" selects a word from the word collection. On paper or the blackboard, he or she draws a line for each letter in the selected word.
3. The other person is the player. The player guesses letters one at a time. If the letter is in the word, "it" writes it in on the correct line or lines. If the letter is not in the word, "it" writes a G (the first letter of *Game Over*) below the lines.
4. Play continues. If the player correctly guesses the word within eight tries, he has won. If not, "it" spells the words *Game Over* letter by letter below the lines, and "it" wins.

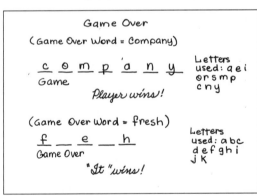

Game Over

❋ Thursday: COMMERCIALLY PRODUCED WORD GAMES

There are many enjoyable games on the market that provide word practice.[2] Although they don't necessarily involve children with the week's word collections, games such as Spill and Spell, Scrabble, Boggle, Balderdash, and Pictionary get children thinking about words and provide practice in using spelling strategies.

SUMMARY

For Thursday activities, word play encourages students to explore words, word meanings, and spelling patterns. Such play is not only fun, it's educational—brain research has shown that we learn more quickly when we are actively engaged in learning.

Playing word games promotes creativity and exploration, both of which enhance learning.

---

2. The book *On a Roll With Spelling* by JoAnne Currah and Jane Felling (authors of the "Boxcars and One-eyed Jacks" math games) has a wealth of games that students can play in partners or small groups. Another source of spelling games we have found useful is *Jellybean Spelling*.

THURSDAY: PERSONAL FAVORITES, NEW AND OLD

THURSDAY: PERSONAL FAVORITES, NEW AND OLD

Thursday: Personal Favorites, New and Old

FRIDAY: SHOWING WHAT WE KNOW

Fridays have traditionally been test days—a time when students show how many words they have memorized over the week. This spelling program asks students to go beyond mere memorization and to develop deeper understandings of the underlying structures, patterns, and relationships within and among words. Therefore, the Friday evaluation activities require students to demonstrate increased knowledge, understanding, and the correct use of words from the week's collection.

KEY POINTS FOR FRIDAY

- There are many ways of demonstrating knowledge—the Friday test is one, but not the only one.
- Focus on what the students do right, rather than what they do wrong. For example, counting the number of letters correct rather than the number of words wrong can give a child and parent a better sense of progress. The child who progresses from spelling *computer* as *cuptor* to spelling it as *cumputer* has made significant growth, from five out of eight letters correct (62.5 percent) to seven out of eight letters correct (87.5 percent).
- Analyzing children's errors provides information that is helpful in planning future spelling instruction. Teaching children to analyze their own error patterns helps them identify their own weaknesses and gain power over their use of spelling strategies.

Step by step

1. Select a Friday activity or choice of activities.
2. Provide students with the necessary direction.
3. Provide adequate time for the activity—usually about twenty to thirty minutes.

Teacher-proven ideas

The following activities work with just about any word collection and any group of students. The difficulty level of the class word collection and the personal word lists determines the difficulty of these activities. Since students have been involved in creating the class word collection and selecting their personal word lists, the difficulty level is usually appropriate.

Word Bees **56**

Peer Tests **57**

Transfer Tally **58**

Prove It! **59**

Self Reports **60**

❋ Friday: WORD BEES

In traditional spelling bees, the student who needed the most practice with spelling was usually the first one out or "spelled down." We have modeled our spelling bees after old-time quilting bees, where groups of people worked together to produce something (and no one ever got "quilted down").

Step by step

1. Use the week's word collection and related words.
2. Four students, numbered one to four, work together as a team.
3. Give a word from the word collection. Allow a few minutes for the groups to be sure each of their members can spell it and its related forms. This is the "bee" part—all working together.
4. Roll a die. If the numbers one through four are rolled, the person in each group with the corresponding number goes to the board; if number five, players one and four go together; if number six, players two and three go together.

5. Give the word or a form of it to the contestants at the board. When more than one person is working together at the board, we give related words. When a single player goes to the board, we give the original word, or the original word with an *s*, *ed*, or *ing* ending added.
6. If a player misses the word, her group can join her at the board and help her fix it.

Word Bees

❋ Friday: PEER TESTS

Peer tests are not new. What's new is the emphasis on word analysis, on working with a partner to try and figure out why mistakes occurred, and on developing strategies to use when spelling these words in the future.

Step by step

1. Partners A and B trade lists. They read through their partner's list to be sure they can read all the words.
2. Reading from B's notebook, A dictates B's word list.
3. B writes the words as they are dictated, in standard spelling-test format.
4. At the end of B's test, the partners switch roles, and B tests A, dictating from A's notebook.
5. At the completion of both tests, the partners reclaim their own notebooks and check their tests.
6. They count the total number of letters and the number of letters correct, and calculate the percentage of letters correct. They then count the number of words and number of words spelled correctly, and calculate that percentage.

Sometimes, you want to give a whole-class spelling test if there is a particular set of words everyone in the class needs to know. Whole-class tests could be based on frequently used and misspelled words, science terms where correct spelling is critical, or the names of classmates.

Friday: Showing What We Know 57

7. Partners then compare their tests, double-checking each others' marking, and search for any patterns to their errors—if they made any!
8. Partners discuss errors and share strategies for figuring out or remembering how to spell words either of them missed.

	Spelling Test	Name Justin Partner Kris Date March 7		
	dictated words	correct spelling	checked by partner	number of letters correct / number of letters in word
1	multiplacation	multiplication	✓	13/14
2	multiply		✓	8/8
3	multaple	multiple	✓	6/7
4	subtract		✓	8/8
5	subtraction		✓	11/11
6	submarene	submarine	✓	8/9
7	substitute		✓	10/10
8	substitution		✓	12/12
9	locate		✓	6/6
10	location		✓	8/8
11	locle	local	✓	3/5
12				
13				
14				
15				
16				
17				
18				

a 94 Total number of letters correct   94 ÷ 99 × 100 = 94.9 %
b 99 Total number of letters   a   b

a 7   Total number of words correct   7 ÷ 11 × 100 = 63.6 %
b 11 Total number of words   a   b

Peer test

🟦 Friday: TRANSFER TALLY

One of the basic goals of any spelling program is to help children spell more conventionally in their written production. This activity assesses progress toward that goal. Word collections based on current classroom activities in science, social studies, themes, or projects work best for this activity.

Step by step

1. Students skim backward and forward through their week's collection of written work, highlighting words from the current word collection and personal word lists. Derivatives and related words count, too.
2. Students tally how many words they have highlighted and how many times these words were spelled correctly.
3. Add the two tally figures to obtain a numerical score. This process recognizes the students' attempts to use the words as well as their ability to spell them correctly.

❋ Friday: PROVE IT!

There are many ways for students to show what they have learned. Sometimes they are better at finding these ways than we are. This activity puts the ownership of demonstrating learning in the hands of the learners.

Step by step

1. Brainstorm with students some ways they could show what they know about this week's word list. Record the information on chart paper for future reference.
2. Tell students they have twenty minutes (or thirty, depending on students' ages and class schedules) to figure out what they have learned about words this week, and to Prove It! using one of the following activities or one of their own ideas.
3. Students present what they have learned about words this week to the class, small group, classroom helper, or teacher.

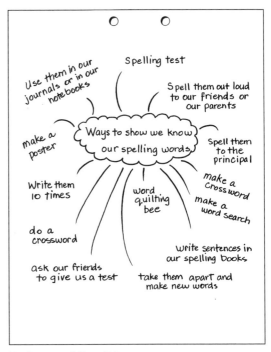

Brainstormed list of ideas for "Prove It!"

Friday: Showing What We Know

❊ Friday: SELF-REPORTS

Spelling is a topic that interests parents. Poor spelling is certain to be a concern, whereas spelling improvement isn't always noticed. One effective strategy is to send students home with evidence of their growth. Copies of journal entries, first and final drafts of reports, and daily assignments can demonstrate student progress. We include a parent response form, designed as a blank form letter from the parent to the student. With this, students are recognized for their accomplishments, and parents have additional input into our spelling program.

Step by step

1. Students select samples of work that show their spelling growth. Teachers can help with this selection if necessary.

Student self-report

2. Students practice sharing their samples and pointing out evidence of their growth with a partner.
3. Students take work samples and parent-response forms home and share them with their parents. Be sure they take a response form for each parent.
4. Students return the samples and response forms and add them to their spelling notebooks.

Name Justin **Date** Nov. 10

Dear Mom and Dad

My spelling is improving! I know this because

1. I got 18/20 words correct on my test that Trisha gave me. (90%)
2. I got 146/149 letters correct on my test. (99%)
3. I learned to remember the spelling of ex-words by remembering that ex is a prefix.

I am proud of myself as a speller because
I used my words in my daily work and spelled them all correctly.

One spelling problem I am working on is words that end in er and or.

You can help me by playing games with me sometimes.

My next spelling goal is to learn to spell words that end in er and or right.

I have attached some spelling work for you to look at

Sincerely, Justin

Date Nov. 13

Dear Justin
           child

Thank you for showing us your spelling work. I/we are impressed by

1. how many words you have learned.
2. how you learn so many more words by adding prefixes and suffixes.
3. your work on word origins and what the different parts mean.

One thing we'd like you to know is
We wish we'd learned to spell this way!

Sincerely Mom & Dad

Dear Mrs. Stewart
           child's teacher

We'd like to let you know that Justin has become much more interested in spelling this year. Thanks!

Thanks Leigh Hambly

Student self-report

SUMMARY

For Friday activities, remember the Friday test is only one way of demonstrating spelling knowledge, and we must always focus on what students do right rather than what they do wrong. By analyzing children's errors we gain information that helps us plan future spelling instruction. Teaching children to analyze their own error patterns helps them identify their own weaknesses and gain power over their use of spelling strategies.

FRIDAY: PERSONAL FAVORITES, NEW AND OLD

FRIDAY: PERSONAL FAVORITES, NEW AND OLD

FRIDAY: PERSONAL FAVORITES, NEW AND OLD

CLASSROOM ROUTINES THAT SUPPORT YOUR SPELLING PROGRAM

There are many routines we use in our classrooms that support our spelling program and extend students' abilities.

KEY POINTS FOR CLASSROOM ROUTINES

- Each one of us is already teaching spelling through the many activities that we do each day. The trick is to recognize and enhance these opportunities for helping our students make sense of words and gain power over their use.
- We know from recent brain research that when we laugh, play, and have fun, the composition of chemicals affecting our brains changes. These changes help our brains make new neural connections that enhance our ability to learn. So the best thing you can do to teach spelling is to wordsmith—have fun creating!

Classroom routines that support spelling

Teacher-proven classroom routines

The following teacher-proven routines can be found in this section:

> Ongoing Assessment **66**
> Writing Process **70**
> Proofreading **71**
> Weekly Edit **73**
> Mystery Message/
>   C.O.P.S./Daily Edits **74**
> Morning News **76**
> Calendar Time **77**
> Password Out the Door **78**
> Weird Word Collections **78**

❋ Classroom Routines: ONGOING ASSESSMENT

At the beginning of the school year and throughout the year, you get to know your students, their abilities in spelling, the strategies they use, and the difficulties they have. Four ways we find effective for gaining this information are

- observing applications of spelling skills
- analyzing errors
- observing students' ability to self-correct
- administering repeated spelling tests

We have used one or more of these approaches, in various combinations, over the years. You may wish to start with one and add others later. We recommend starting by observing your students' application of spelling skills. This takes very little time and provides information that reflects the goal of any spelling program—improvement in spelling in written work. When you are comfortable with it, add another ongoing assessment technique.

APPLICATION OF SPELLING SKILLS

To observe students' application of spelling skills, keep copies of students' unedited drafts and final copies of written work in a file or portfolio. Over time, progress becomes apparent when you compare the works. This assessment reflects the goal of this spelling program; that is, to improve children's spelling in their written work.

Step by step

1. Photocopy a page from the student's journal or other unedited work once a month.
2. Place the copies in the student's portfolio or individual file.
3. Review the collected pages two or three times a year as part of ongoing assessment.
4. Note improvements. For some students, improvement may mean that they are no longer confusing *to, too,* and *two*. For others, it may mean that they are correctly determining when to double consonants before adding suffixes.

This collection can be useful as part of a student-teacher, parent-teacher, or parent-student-teacher conference. Growth in spelling and writing ability is usually apparent over time, without any specific analysis.

ERROR ANALYSIS

Another way to determine your students' needs is to do an ongoing error analysis using students' unedited work. You can use the same material collected for the "application of spelling skills" assessment.

Step by step

1. Select a page or two of the student's writing. Journals work well for this.
2. Make a list of the misspelled words in the selected pages on an error analysis sheet.
3. Analyze the errors (e.g., suffix errors, contractions, vowel errors), and note any patterns.
4. Repeat every two or three months. Some teachers like to do this prior to each reporting period as part of their spelling assessment. Others teach their students to do

their own error analysis and include these self-analysis forms in the students' portfolios or individual files.

5. If you find a number of students making the same kinds of errors, you can use that information in planning for future weeks' word study.

Error Analysis Sheet

Name: michael

Date	Word	Vowel	Consonant	Word Middle	Suffix/Prefix	3C's*	Silent Letters	Meaning	Letter Order
Sept. 15	Wensday / Wednesday			x			x		
	holaday / holiday	x							
	runing / running		x		x				
	theif / thief	x					x		x
	sine / sign						x	x	
Nov. 12	wasent / wasn't					x			
	devision / division	x							
	forgeting / forgetting		x		x				
	Thanksgivin / Thanksgiving		x					x	
March	febuary / february			x				x	
	there / they're					x		x	

*3C's = Contractions, Compounds, and Conundrums

Error Analysis Sheet

ABILITY TO SELF-CORRECT

A third assessment focuses on students' ability to self-correct their own written products. Proofreading/correcting written work is an important skill, and one that students need practice to develop. A process approach to writing instruction supports development of this skill.

Step by step

1. Students select a first draft piece from their journal, writing portfolio, or other unedited work.

68 Building Connections: WORDSMITHING

2. Students independently proofread and correct the spelling in the piece, using available resources such as dictionaries, textbooks, and class word lists.
3. Both the first drafts and the corrected drafts are photocopied and placed in the students' portfolios or individual files.
4. Repeat two or three times a year.

REPEATED SPELLING TEST

Another way to do a class assessment is to administer the same spelling test three or four times over the course of the year. We select twenty misspelled words from our students' written work in September and create a short paragraph or poem for the test. Some teachers prefer to use a grade-leveled, commercially prepared spelling test.

Step by step

1. Create the spelling test. The words can be selected from a grade-leveled spelling text (most schools still have these around somewhere), standardized test, or list of high-frequency or frequently misspelled words. Better yet, you can develop the list in September by selecting misspelled words from your students' written work. Add a short dictation component, such as a poem, a paragraph from the social studies text, or a paragraph you have created using words you want your students to learn.
2. Give the test to your class as you would any regular spelling test. Do not give them words or dictation to study ahead of time.
3. Collect and mark the tests. Don't return or discuss the test results with the students (other than to explain to them that the tests provide you with planning information and document the class's improvement in spelling over time).
4. File the tests in your spelling assessment file, or in the students' individual files.
5. Repeat the test once every three or four months. Compare to previous tests.

❋ Classroom Routines: WRITING PROCESS

The writing process (or the process approach to writing) involves children collecting ideas, drafting, revising, proofreading, and publishing—a method of writing many adult writers use. Publishing may be as simple as posting a finished piece on the bulletin board or as elaborate as producing a book containing an individual student's (or student group's) writing. Students involved in the writing process often keep journals; collections of "timed-writes" or "quick-writes" for future ideas; and portfolios of ideas, completed works, and drafts in progress. This process has been described in detail by a number of authors.[1]

Step by step

1. Encourage children to use temporary spelling when drafting.
2. Encourage children to get as much of a word down as they can on their own when drafting—first sounds, last sounds, syllables or word parts, prefixes, endings—any parts they remember or can figure out.
3. Discourage stopping midprocess to look up words or to ask for help from others (including the teacher).
4. Teach children to do what adult writers often do—if unsure of a word, simply note *SP?* beside or above it and carry on with the writing.
5. Talk about the differences between composing and editing, editing and proofreading, and how trying to pay attention to too many things at once interferes with doing a good job of the task at hand.
6. Discuss and reinforce the idea that the message comes first and fixing up comes later.

---

[1]. Three books we found particularly helpful are *In the Middle*, by Nancie Atwell; *Transitions*, by Regie Routman; and *Creating Classrooms for Authors*, by Jerome Harste and Kathy Short. All are published by Heinemann.

✹ Classroom Routines: PROOFREADING

Proofreading is the final part of editing. When proofreading, writers focus on the surface aspects of their writing, including punctuation, capitalization, and spelling. This is ordinarily done after students have made initial revisions to content and wording. Proofreading is an integral part of the writing process when the writing is meant to be shared with others.

Students often don't have any idea how to systematically approach proofreading. Teach them the following steps with their own writing, or teach them a proofreading strategy that works for you. The aim is to help students develop independence as writers and to take control of their own corrections.

Step by step

1. Have students read their draft, marking questionable words with an *SP?*.
2. Have them read it again, backwards, from bottom to top, last word to first, marking questionable words with an *SP?*.
3. Tell students to try two or three different spellings of marked words in the margins of their draft.
4. Suggest they use one of the spellings if it looks right.
5. If none of the spellings looks right, suggest they pick the one they think is closest. Have them look it up in the dictionary or the last place they might have seen it (e.g., the science text), or try it on the spell checker. Tell them to keep trying different spellings and/or different resources until they find the correct one.
6. If this doesn't work, suggest students ask someone else, then double-check in the dictionary.
7. Have students write the correct spelling in their draft and thoroughly cross out the misspelling.
8. Have them highlight the correct spelling, and highlight the part they had trouble with in another color of highlighter.
9. When they are finished proofreading and correcting, have students write each corrected word in the personal words section of their spelling notebook.

10. Have them highlight trouble spots.
11. Ask students to take a few seconds to think about each word and how they might remember it in future. Is it part of a known word family? Is there a mnemonic device that might help them remember it? Does it have a special shape or other interesting feature?

Steps 9 to 11 could be done later as a Tuesday, Wednesday, or Friday spelling activity.

Name: Ardy Smith	From: Wordsmithing draft	
Words Misspelled	**Correction**	**Comments**
nmemonic	mnemonic	Remember - the m is first for memory
calender	calendar	Spell-checker found this one - a typo. er doesn't look right.
to	too	Careless error - found it proofreading backwards
occured	occurred	Double-checked the spelling on these. Never sure about double consonants
occassional	occasional	
favourites	favorites	Canadian & American spellings - Using American this time and forgot.
colours	colors	
graffitti	graffiti	sp? Try exaggerated pronunciation - graf fee tee to remember 2 f's, one t.
exagerated	exaggerated	Didn't look right with one g - had to look it up. Remember - it means excessive and two g's is excessive.

Proofreading analysis from Ardy's *Wordsmithing* draft.

❄ Classroom Routines: WEEKLY EDIT

Weekly Edit is a group editing activity, using one student's first draft of a piece of writing.

How to do Weekly Edit, step by step:

1. Note common problems children are having with their writing. We do this informally as we observe children writing in their journals, doing quick-writes, or working on projects or assignments.
2. From student writing samples, select a draft that contains errors you can use to teach about these common problems.
3. Get the student author's permission to use the piece.
4. Photocopy one or two paragraphs of the piece on an overhead transparency.
5. Display the piece and proofread it as a group, making corrections on the transparency as needed. Do as much as you can in ten to twenty minutes. It isn't necessary to do the whole piece.
6. The student who volunteered his work now has a head start on his editing and you have had an opportunity to teach a number of short lessons on your students' writing problems. We have tackled everything from how many humps an *m* has in cursive to the use of hyphens in two-word adjectives. We only teach things that we've identified through children's writing—that is our "text."

Ways to enhance spelling through Weekly Edit, step by step:

1. Discuss spelling errors identified during the edit, and strategies that could be applied to spelling the words correctly. This way, teacher and students share their knowledge of spelling strategies and reveal the thinking behind them.
2. Select a few correctly spelled words, and encourage the author to describe how she knew the correct spelling. Often the answer is simply, "It looked right." In this case, probe for more information, with such questions as "Where have you seen this word before? Do you

> Read a piece aloud to a student's parents without letting them see the text. This can be an effective way to demonstrate a child's writing ability to parents who have become stuck on the child's spelling problems.

remember consciously thinking about it? Do you know other related words?"

3. Talk about words, spelling strategies, and how we know how to spell. Encourage students to share their insights. Some children are amazed to discover that there is more to spelling than just sounding out.
4. Encourage positive input from everyone, using the Weekly Edit as an example of group problem solving.
5. Discuss the difference between composition and spelling. Explain that some people are very good at creating such things as stories and reports but need extra help with spelling and other mechanics of writing.
6. Occasionally read a draft to the class. Focus on the qualities of the piece—the writing style, meaning, language—before putting part of it on the overhead to proofread. This is especially effective for children who are good writers but who have difficulties with spelling

❋ Classroom Routines: MYSTERY MESSAGES/ C.O.P.S./ DAILY EDITS

Mystery messages are messages the teacher writes on the board in cloze format. The message, directed to the students, is often humorous, or it relates to current classroom activities or community events. The mystery message becomes a C.O.P.S. (Capitalization, Omissions, Punctuation, Spelling) activity when the teacher purposefully includes errors of those four types. Some children may be overwhelmed with a combined mystery and C.O.P.S. message, so you may want to do two separate messages. Daily Edits are messages the teacher writes on the board. These messages can include a variety of errors, including incorrect usage, tenses, spellings, homophones—any errors that exemplify a language skill you wish to teach. *Multi-age and More* (Politano and Davies 1994) provides more information on these and similar activities.

Step by step

1. Create a mystery message using words, word families, and/or spelling patterns from the current word collection.
2. Include frequently misspelled words you have identified from your students' written work.
3. Mystery messages can be solved by the whole class, or students can work individually to solve the mystery. When working individually, students copy the message into their notebooks, completing and correcting as they go.
4. Follow up with a discussion of how the puzzle was solved.
5. Teach the terms *synonym* and *antonym* as you discuss words that could be used to solve the mystery message. (Students often insert synonyms, and occasionally antonyms, for the actual word you had deleted from the message.)
6. Teach the terms and concepts *noun, verb, adjective, adverb,* and any other parts of speech that are appropriate for your grade level, as you discuss words for the mystery message.
7. Provide opportunities for students to create mystery messages for each other or for other classes.

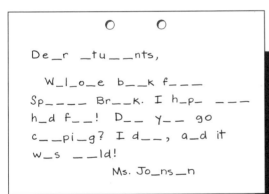

Mystery message

C.O.P.S. message

Classroom Routines That Support Your Spelling Program

Daily Edit message

good morning did you have to shovel your walk this a m befor you come to school. the snowe was vary deep at me and my husbands' house. Hour children haved to help us shovelle the driveway so we can drive to work this morning the whetherman said it willn't melt until nevt weak.

Good morning. Did you have to shovel your walk this a.m. before you came to school? The snow was very deep at my husband's and my house. Our children had to help us shovel the driveway so we could drive to work this morning. The weather forecaster said it won't melt until next week.

Note: In the daily edit example shown, "this morning" can either end one sentence or begin the next. This teacher likes to use this trick to show that there are lots of different ways to be right and to get students talking about sentence structure.

❉ Classroom Routines: MORNING NEWS

Morning News is a time for children to contribute school, community, and family news. As children share this, the teacher writes the news on the board, asking for help with spelling, punctuation, and sentence structure. Some teachers designate a student to copy the news onto a news sheet each day. This can then be photocopied and sent home to parents on Friday.

Step by step

1. Encourage individuals, small groups, or the whole class to spell out words as you write.
2. Discuss words that are difficult, unusual, represent familiar spelling patterns or word families, or can be remembered using a mnemonic device. (For example, if your morning news involves the school principal, you could use something like, "Ms. Birdwell, our principal, is our pal").
3. Identify any homophones (words that sound alike but are spelled differently, e.g., *hear* and *here*, *blew* and *blue*),

homographs (words that are spelled alike but sound different, e.g., "I won't *read* this book because I already *read* it"), or homonyms (words that are the same but have different meanings, e.g., "I had to *duck* when the *duck* flew over me"). Compare the pairs of words.
4. Select one or two words from the morning news and play with them. Brainstorm for possible prefixes, suffixes, different tenses, plural or singular forms. Think of other words with a shared spelling pattern or from the same word family.

❋ Classroom Routines: CALENDAR TIME

Most primary teachers and many intermediate teachers have a regular calendar time each morning, which is part of opening exercises or group time. This is a good opportunity for short lessons in language arts and math, as discussion centers around days, months, and past, present, and future activities. Although many people consider calendar time to be a primary activity, it can be further developed for intermediate students by adding more sophisticated weather words, discussions of the origins of day and month names, and a "This day in history" component.

Step by step

1. Chant spellings of the month and day names.
2. Cover the calendar and have children write the full date on the board (e.g., Friday, September 20, 1996). This can be done at students' desks on slates or scratch paper if there isn't enough room at the board for all to work at once.
3. Discuss the origin of the name of the month and day. Look it up together, or assign it as a mini–research project.
4. Play with "silly" or overly precise pronunciations of the names to help remember spellings: Wed-nes-day, Feb-ru-ary.
5. Create mnemonic devices (e.g., "Sunday is a fun day but Monday is not") to remember the *u* and *o* spellings.

6. Use calendar time to explore weather words for the day, holiday names and their origins, and special activities associated with each day.

❖ Classroom Routines: PASSWORD OUT THE DOOR

Password Out the Door is a game in which children have to supply a password to leave the room for recess, lunch, or at the end of the day. The password may be a commonly misspelled word, a synonym, a fact or date, a math fact, or any brief piece of information that you want children to commit to memory. As children prepare to leave the room, they whisper the password to you or write it on a slate or the chalkboard. This is done in great secrecy. Passwords we have used include such things as the answer to 8 times 7, the correct spelling of *they*, any synonym for the word *nice*, or any three words from the *ight* family.

Step by step

1. Select as a password a frequently misspelled word from children's writing—one you can't stand to see one more time (e.g., *thay* for *they*).
2. Have a special place on the board for the day's password. Put it up first thing in the morning, perhaps as part of Morning News or calendar activities.
3. Introduce the password. Explain why you selected it, and discuss any information you have on its origin, spelling pattern, or word family.
4. If students misspell the password, quietly direct them to look at it again and come back.

❖ Classroom Routines: WEIRD WORD COLLECTION

This collection is made up of words that don't seem to fit the spelling patterns of similar words. Unlike the words in the weekly class word collections, these words are collected over a number of weeks. When thirty or forty have been collected, this set of words can be used as a class collection.

Different classes have come up with a variety of names for this list—Misfits, Quirks, Mavericks, Doozers, Outlaws, Erratics, or just plain Weird Words. Have fun naming your list with your class.

Step by step

1. Create a space for the Weird Word Collection. This can be a sheet of chart paper, butcher paper taped to the wall, or a specially designed bulletin board. We have used a "dragon" bulletin board and put new words on "scales" created out of colored construction paper from the scrap box.
2. Any words that come up during Monday word collection activities that don't quite fit the pattern or family under study (but seem like they should) can be added to this list. For example, *height* might be added when the *eigh* pattern is being collected because it doesn't follow the pattern for pronunciation.
3. Students also add words they find during their studies in other curricular areas. Often, foreign and technical words from social studies and science end up on this list, for example, *mosquito, pharoah, Kiev, tsunami*.
4. When this set of words is chosen as the week's class collection, discuss when and why each word was added to the list. Brainstorm for other words that share the same weird spelling patterns as the words in the collection.

SUMMARY

For classroom routines, remember that each one of us is already teaching spelling through the many activities that we do throughout the day. Recognize and enhance these opportunities.

CLASSROOM ROUTINES: PERSONAL FAVORITES, NEW AND OLD

CLASSROOM ROUTINES: PERSONAL FAVORITES, NEW AND OLD

CLASSROOM ROUTINES: PERSONAL FAVORITES, NEW AND OLD

EVALUATION

Many of us have memories of the spelling star chart, where everyone's spelling expertise (or lack of it) was displayed for all to see. Those children for whom spelling came easily were rewarded and those for whom spelling was difficult were chastised publicly. As Alfie Kohn (1994) has forcefully pointed out in his book, *Punished by Rewards*, such reward systems teach children who do well that they don't have to try, and teach those who don't do well that, no matter how hard they *do* try, they still aren't smart enough to "get it!" When the pursuit of perfection becomes more important than the learning itself, we are in danger of teaching children how to do well in school rather than well in life. Spelling for the test is not a life skill; spelling for communication is—and one that can't be tested with twenty words each week.

The purpose of spelling evaluation is to provide information for planning of instruction, to inform students about their progress, and to collect data for communicating and reporting to parents. The purpose of collecting data is to show student learning. Students show this learning when they

- demonstrate what they are able to do (observation of process)
- reflect on their learning and evaluate themselves (reflection)
- collect samples of their spelling to show what they know (observation of product)

Teachers who watch students at work, collect samples of students' spelling, and help children self-assess, are able to make thoughtful observations of student spellers in a variety of contexts. This not only yields the information they need to plan instruction but also to assess and evaluate student learning in spelling[1].

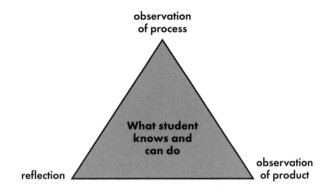

KEY POINTS FOR EVALUATION

- When evaluating spelling, look for what the student can do before deciding what needs to be learned.
- Involve students in self-evaluation and in peer evaluation. This gives them lots of practice assessing what they and their peers can do and what strategies need to be learned.
- Take "repeated measures over time." This involves repeating the same assessment two or three times throughout the term and comparing the results. Then compare these findings with your observations and the students' self-evaluations. This is particularly valuable when trying to determine why an unexpectedly poor speller is having problems.

---

1. This perspective arises from the work of Lincoln and Guba (1984) and others. These ways of evaluating are demonstrated in *Together is Better: Collaborative Assessment, Evaluation, and Reporting* (Davies et al. 1990).

Teacher-proven evaluation ideas

The following ideas have proven useful for assessing and evaluating spelling:

    Ways to Collect and Organize Spelling Data 85
    Spelling Analysis 86
    Reflecting on Learning 88
    Setting Criteria 90
    Strategies Good Spellers Use 91

❋ Evaluation: WAYS TO COLLECT AND ORGANIZE SPELLING DATA

Information about your students' learning can be collected in any way that makes sense to you. Be sure your students assist with the collecting and organizing of data about their spelling growth. They need to know how well they are doing so they can be buoyed by their successes. They must also focus their energies in the areas that need work and be able to explain their spelling growth and progress to their parents.

Remember to keep your record-keeping system *simple*! You only need to select one or two ways that work for you.

Data collection grid with space for each student

Evaluation 85

Some ways we have found valuable are

- data collection grids
- binders with sections for each child
- library pocket charts
- large grid or file folder system with post-it notes or labels affixed to record observations
- checklists
- student notebooks

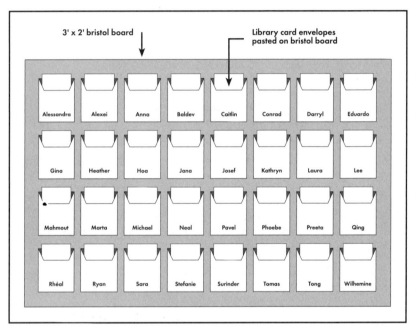

Library pocket charts, wall-mounted

❋ Evaluation: SPELLING ANALYSIS

When children review their own spelling production and look for words they can spell correctly, words they need to correct, and the strategies they use to find correct spellings, they begin to bring the spelling of words under their power and become responsible spellers. Completing surveys that focus students' attention on the strategies they use helps students become aware of what they do when they spell.

Step by step
1. Prepare a spelling survey for students. Use the sample shown, or create your own using the guidelines below.
2. Ask students to choose a piece of writing (e.g., journal, writing folder, research project) and record on the form the first nine words they spelled correctly.
3. Next, have them record on the form the first nine words they spelled wrong.
4. Then ask students to check one another's lists and initial them.
5. Have them answer the remaining questions.
6. Collect the completed forms, review, and ask students to file them in their personal folders.

When creating your survey, consider including the following questions:
1. Do you see any patterns or similarities in the words you've misspelled?
2. Do most of your misspellings involve vowels (*a, e, i, o, u,* and sometimes *y*)?
3. Do most of your misspellings involve "schwa" vowels? (Schwa vowels, such as the *a* in *afraid,* the *e* in *system,* the *i* in *pencil,* the *o* in *correct,* and the *u* in *success,* occur in the unaccented syllable.)
4. Do any of your misspellings occur in words with prefixes (e.g., *dis, im, non*), suffixes (e.g., *tion, ily, ence*), or inflectional endings (e.g., *s, es, ed,* and *ing*)?
5. Are most of the spelling errors at the beginning, middle, or end of words?
6. Do most of your misspellings occur in long words or in short words? Is there any pattern to the number of syllables in the words you missed?
7. Are most of the words you misspelled frequently used words, or unusual words?

Other questions:
- What is the hardest word you know how to spell?
- What is the most interesting word you know?
- What word would you like to learn how to spell?

➤ What word would your teacher like you to learn how to spell?
➤ What part of spelling drives you crazy?

Spelling Analysis

Name _____ Date _____
Checked by _____
The piece of work I'm analyzing is _____
_____

Words Spelled Correctly

1. _____ 4. _____ 7. _____
2. _____ 5. _____ 8. _____
3. _____ 6. _____ 9. _____

Spelling Errors

1. _____ 4. _____ 7. _____
                                8. _____
                                9. _____

> The hardest word I know how to spell is Wednesday.
> It is hard because you can't hear the d.
> The most interesting word I know how to spell is humongous.
> It is interesting because we couldn't find it in the dictionary.
> I'd like you to know I like getting to make the list to take home. to do with my mom and some of them are my words.
>
> signed: Justin

Personal spelling analysis

Reproducible master in Appendix

✣ Evaluation: REFLECTING ON LEARNING

When we encourage students to think about the ways they spell, they can make valuable insights. Students begin to identify the strategies that help them spell and the roadblocks that impede them. Reflection also helps students acknowledge their learning. Acknowledging one's own accomplishments makes for more confident learners—learners who take risks with their spelling in order to learn more about language.

The four reflection frames shown have been developed by teachers and are useful for student self-reflection.

Reflection frames

Frame 1:
Name _____
Date _____
This piece of work shows _____
The hardest word for me to spell was _____ because _____

Frame 2:
Name _____
Date _____
When you are looking at the spelling in this story please notice that:
1. _____
2. _____

Frame 3:
Name _____
Date _____
When we were building our Spelling Spines I was surprised to learn that _____
This surprised me because _____

Frame 4: Spelling Compliments
I would like to give myself the following spelling compliments

Reflection frames

Step by step

1. Give a copy of the Spelling Profile of the Week (right) to each student.
2. Have the students fill it in as a Friday activity.
3. Repeat this activity on a regular basis and store sheets in spelling folders.
4. Periodically ask students to review sheets completed over time and note any patterns that are developing.

Spelling Profile of the Week

Name _____
Date _____

My word list for this week
_____

I selected these words because _____

During the week I learned these three interesting facts about my words _____

I had to really work hard to learn these words _____

The best part of spelling this week was _____

My spelling goal for next week is _____ because _____

Spelling profile of the week

Evaluation 89

❋ Evaluation: SETTING CRITERIA

When students help develop the criteria for an assignment or learning activity, they come to understand the expectations we have of them. We learn about their ability to show what they know in various forms, such as a research project, a presentation, a written essay, or science experiment. When we build criteria for written work, we often include a section for mechanics, such as spelling and punctuation. Sometimes students who are knowledgeable in the subject area yet are poor spellers, do poorly, because their spelling ends up counting for more than their knowledge. It is important to provide both a spelling assessment and a knowledge assessment so poor spellers are not unfairly penalized. One teacher, with her students,

Procedures Checklist
for checking spelling and writing con[ventions]

- ☐ read text forward to proofread and edit
- ☐ read backward to proofread
- ☐ read by peer out loud to me
- ☐ spell checker used
- ☐ capital letter corrections made
- ☐ punctuation corrected
- ☐ variety of punctuation used (: , ; , " " ( ))
- ☐ handwriting legible/legible text
- ☐ illustrations labelled neatly
- ☐ cover/title page
- ☐ Other: _____

See over for spelling checklist.

Procedures checklist

Spelling and Writing Conventions Checklist

Name __Mac Guelph__ Date __Jan. 15, 1997__
For __My Digestive System__

Criteria	Student Mac	Peer Sam	Teacher Mrs. L.
correct spelling	✓	✓	✓
correct use of punctuation	✓	✓	✓
correct capitalization	✓	✓	✓
correct formatting	✓	✓	✓
neat presentation	✓	✓	✓
legible text	✓	✓	✓
Other: illustrations labelled neatly	✓	✓	well done, Mac!

✓ Yes ✗ No N/A Not Applicable
See over for procedures list.

Spelling and writing checklist

Reproducible masters in Appendix

90 Building Connections: WORDSMITHING

developed the criteria shown for students to use whenever they handed in a project or assignment for grading. She gave them copies of the procedures checklist to put in their notebooks for frequent reference. She also provided parents with a copy of both the spelling and procedure checklists, printed back to back, so they would understand the process used.

❋ Evaluation: STRATEGIES GOOD SPELLERS USE

When we ask students what good spellers do, we begin to understand the strategies they understand and have available to use. We then document that information and use it to shape our teaching. When we revisit the list with our students over the course of the year, we have a record of their growth and understanding as spellers. This list also acts as a source of ideas and strategies for students to use when self-assessing or when they are stuck on a spelling.

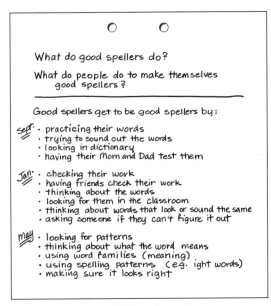

Criteria list. This is added to three times a year

SUMMARY

When evaluating spelling, remember: look for what the students can do before deciding what needs to be learned; involve students in self-evaluation and in peer evaluation; repeat assessment measures over time and compare results.

Evaluation: Personal Favorites, New and Old

EVALUATION: PERSONAL FAVORITES, NEW AND OLD

Evaluation: Personal Favorites, New and Old

INVITING, INCLUDING, AND INFORMING OTHERS

As we work with our students, we need to invite, include, and inform others. Then they can understand the kind of spelling program we offer and be supportive of our students' learning. Involving parents and others in our spelling program can help us learn about their children as spellers. We can also give them enough information to reassure them that effective spelling instruction is taking place in our classroom.

Many of our students' parents recall their less-than-positive spelling experiences at school, and these memories color their reactions. Parents are anxious that their children experience success. If parents are good spellers, they may not appreciate the world of a poor speller; they believe that their child could do better if he or she "only worked harder." This is just one of many views about spelling, which are as varied as the individuals who hold them. For this reason it is important that we inform parents and others about spelling and spelling instruction. We do this in ways that are comfortable for us as teachers, helpful to our students as learners, and understandable to parents and our school community.

KEY POINTS FOR INVITING, INCLUDING, AND INFORMING OTHERS

- Involve other people in your students' enjoyment of wordsmithing.
- Invite conversation with others about your spelling program to build support.
- Parents can provide teachers with valuable information both for individual student program design and for planning future communications home.

 **Teacher-proven ideas**

In this chapter we share a few successful ways of inviting, including, and informing others:

> Helping Parents Help With Spelling Homework 96
> Spell-a-bration 97
> Spelling Games Family Night 98
> Spelling Newsletters 101

✣ Inviting, Including, and Informing Others: HELPING PARENTS HELP WITH SPELLING HOMEWORK

Spelling is one school subject nearly all parents are able to provide some help with at home. The following letter informs parents about ways they can support their child's spelling at home.

If you choose Tuesday

- help your child focus on the order of sounds and letters i[n] turns with your child saying parts of the word. For exam[ple] *information*, the exercise would go
  CHILD: in
  PARENT: for
  CHILD: ma
  PARENT: tion

- using letters from a scrabble game (or letters on small squ[ares] a word, scramble the letters, and invite your child to figu[re] put the letters in the correct order. Then have them do th[e]

If you choose Wednesday

- make up your own systems for remembering words, for the end"
- search out all the ways you can change a word by addi[ng] (suffixes) or new beginnings (prefixes), for example, happ[y]

If you choose Thursday

- play word games such as Game Over (Hangman with a n[ew]), Spill and Spell, and Pictionary
- give your child a practice spelling test. After taking the te[st] your child compares what he or she has written with the you can both try to figure out why any mistakes occurre[d]

If you choose Friday

- celebrate the number of words and the number of letters y[our child got right] on his/her test or other Friday activity
- relax and enjoy one another's company at the end of a [week]

Thank you for being so supportive of your child's learning any questions for me please do not hesitate to call.

Best wishes,

Dear Parent(s)/Guardian(s):

Spelling is important. It is valued not only in our classroom but in the world at large. While some people are excellent spellers and spelling is easy for them, others have lots of difficulty spelling. The key to easier spelling for these students is to help them understand why different words are spelled the way they are. We want to put them at ease with words so they enjoy using them.

Here is an overview of our weekly spelling program:

Monday	Collecting the Words (20 minutes)
Tuesday	Taking a Closer Look (10-20 minutes)
Wednesday	Making Sense of Words (10-20 minutes)
Thursday	Playing with Words (20 minutes)
Friday	Showing What We Know (20-30 minutes)

Many parents ask how they can help their son or daughter at home. I recognize that, in today's world, everyone is extremely busy and finding a specific night of the week to work with your child is not always possible. With our program, you can select any night during the week to spend ten minutes helping your children improve their spelling. Please try to schedule a few minutes on Monday evenings or Tuesday mornings to read through your child's word list for the week. (These words are taken from our studies this year, with each week's word list having a different emphasis). As well, please sign your child's spelling contract form.

If you choose Monday

Read the list and sign the contract form. If you have more time, you could
- discuss words on list
- brainstorm related words

Reproducible masters in Appendix

Letter to parents

✳ Inviting, Including, and Informing Others:
SPELL-A-BRATION

If learning to spell is important, then it is important that we celebrate our accomplishments. One teacher, whose class loved words, decided to shift the focus of Valentine's Day to a day her class celebrated words—and not just Valentine's Day words. She suggested to her class that Valentine's Day could be "We Love Words" Day. Preparations, which took place over a two-week period, occurred in art, theme, and free time. They planned the festivities as follows:

1. The class brainstormed all of their favorite words on the board.
2. Children worked in pairs and, with great artistic flair, transferred words onto hearts. They displayed these on their personal bulletin boards.
3. Teacher divided the class's hallway display space; she then divided the class into corresponding small groups. These groups planned how to decorate their section of the hallway bulletin board, shared their plan with their classmates, and had their plan approved by the teacher. Students had a day and an evening to gather the materials. The teacher provided time during the week for each group to do their displays.
4. On Monday of the week before "We Love Words" Day, each child selected the twenty words they loved the most for their weekly word collection. They worked with those words all week. From their collections, students created activities that their classmates and guests could play on "We Love Words" Day.
5. On the Tuesday of the week before "We Love Words" Day, children wrote an invitation to their parents. They asked parents to bring a bag lunch to school on "We Love Words" Day and join them in playing with words over the lunch break.

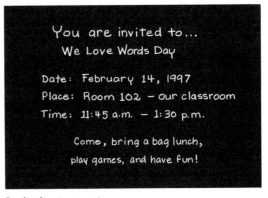

Invitation to parents

This could also be an evening activity. Choose what works best for your school community.

6. Just before lunch time on "We Love Words" Day, the students tidied their room, set up the tables and chairs, and prepared to welcome their families.
7. Families arrived, ate lunch with the children, and then played word games and did word activities that the children had prepared. Before leaving, parents were asked to fill in two compliment cards, one for the class and one for their child.

Dear _____

We really liked

1. _____
  _____
  _____

2. _____
  _____
  _____
  _____

Compliment card

❋ Inviting, Including, and Informing Others: SPELLING GAMES FAMILY NIGHT

On family nights, all family members are invited to school to learn and play together. In our experience, these nights are well attended and get rave reviews from all participants. One teacher decided that she wanted her students' parents to understand her spelling program and learn some new ways to support spelling at home. The family spelling night proceeded as follows:

Step by step

1. Teacher talked about the plan with her students.
2. Students suggested some activities that would be enjoyable to their family members. They determined the activities that were suitable for both younger siblings as well as for older relatives, such as parents and grandparents. They talked about refreshments. (We suggest having families contribute snacks, refreshments, and

personal plastic glasses—enough for their group only. Otherwise, you'll be overwhelmed with food!)
3. Together students and teachers designed an invitation on the chalkboard.
4. Children copied and decorated the invitation to their family and took it home one week in advance.
5. On the day before the Family Spelling night the students wrote a reminder to their families in their home learning log.
6. On the day of the event the teacher and students finalized the agenda and prepared the room.

The evening proceeded as follows:
- Teacher welcomed families.
- Teacher outlined agenda for the evening.
- Children taught family members three games.
- Teacher was available for questions and comments.
- Potluck refreshments were shared.

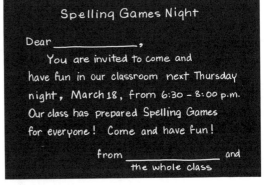

Invitation

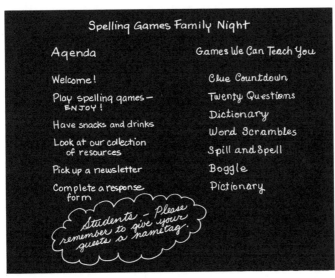

Agenda

Inviting, Including, and Informing Others   99

- Newsletter was distributed (see page 101).
- Parents completed response forms before leaving.

Hints for family nights:
- Invite all family members, including grandparents, older and younger siblings, as well as friends and neighbors.
- Display favorite resource books (with ordering information) and recommended commercial games.
- Have a comprehensive handout or newsletter that includes information about your spelling program and a list of resources for parents.

> Dear *Sheena*
> child's name
>
> Two things I really enjoyed tonight were:
>
> 1. *playing Boggle with you — you are quick!*
>
> 2. *seeing all the spelling stuff you are learning.*
>
> One wish I have is *that we could play games like this at home more often.*
>
> I'd really like you to know that *you are terrific!*
>
> *Thanks, Ms. M — the time it takes for you to have a night like this — it's terrific! Anne*
>
> Love from *Mom & Dad*

Parent response form

✣ Inviting, Including, and Informing Others: SPELLING NEWSLETTERS

Newsletters help keep busy parents up-to-date with classroom programs and their own child's learning. As teachers, it is important that parents receive current information and classroom news efficiently. Yet we have to be careful to balance our need to inform parents with the needs of our students and ourselves.

One teacher prepared this newsletter and saved the document on her word processor. Each year she updates the information and reprints it. Some years her students are responsible for part of the newsletter production. The task then becomes a student responsibility, while the teacher ensures quality of the product.

Another way to develop a newsletter is to make each member of the class responsible for a section. When the master is completed, it is copied and sent home with each student. Newsletters produced in this way become a class publishing activity rather than a weekend-destroying activity for the teacher.

Newsletter

Inviting, Including, and Informing Others

SUMMARY

Remember, when inviting, including, and informing others, to involve other people in your students' enjoyment of wordsmithing.

You build support for your spelling program when you invite conversation with others, and can gain valuable information both for individual student program design and for planning future communications home.

INVITING, INCLUDING, AND INFORMING OTHERS: PERSONAL FAVORITES, NEW AND OLD

INVITING, INCLUDING, AND INFORMING OTHERS: PERSONAL FAVORITES, NEW AND OLD

Questions Parents and Teachers Ask

Why don't children spell as well as they did when I was young?

First of all, we are not sure that they don't spell as well as they used to. We know one reason it appears they don't spell as well is that we encourage them to use a wider range of words at a much earlier age. So rather than writing about Dick and Jane at the farm, as we did, they might be writing about astronauts on Saturn, or Egyptian mummies and pharaohs. Because they are using more interesting and complex words in their writing, they are more likely to make spelling errors.

There is also some indication that as children read less and spend more time watching television and videos, or playing computer games, their exposure to print decreases. We know that reading is one way that most people gain familiarity with how words look and are spelled.

My son brings home stories he has written filled with spelling errors. Why aren't these errors corrected? He keeps repeating the same mistakes and never learns to spell.

As part of the writing process, many teachers encourage their students to do a large number of rough drafts of possible stories—only a few of these will be selected for editing, polishing, and publication. Because we understand how the brain pays attention to things, we encourage students to separate the story-writing process from the editing and proofreading process. In other words, we tell them to get their ideas down first without stopping. If they stop to look words up, it breaks their train of thought, and they lose their story line. Once the ideas are down, students can go back and fix any work worth keeping.

These rough drafts are important for teachers. They offer one source of information about how well students are spelling and what types of words need to be included for formal spelling instruction.

When I was in school we learned to spell by writing out our words to practice them. When we made mistakes, we wrote out our corrections. Why don't teachers have students practice their spelling?

Every time students write they are practicing their spelling. This is one reason we encourage students to write a lot rather than routinely fill in one or two words on a blank worksheet. There is no research evidence that writing words over and over in isolation helps children remember how to spell them in the context of their written work. Instead, we spend more time learning about words—why they are spelled the way they are—rather than in trying to memorize words. (There are roughly two hundred and fifty thousand English words in common usage. Even if we learned twenty words a week, a lifetime is not long enough to memorize all of them.)

Doesn't everyone teach spelling? My other child is in grade one and uses something she calls "invented spelling." What is going to happen to her if no one ever corrects her misspellings?

When young children begin to try to express their ideas in writing, they experiment with words and letters. This experimenting helps them develop ways of thinking about how words are spelled. They begin to recognize common spelling patterns, to pay attention to the relationship between letters and sounds and the way they are ordered in words. When you look at your grade-one child's writing, try to look past the errors and see what your child knows about spelling. For example, even if a word isn't spelled correctly it may have four out of five letters correct—80 percent right. That's an accomplishment that needs to be recognized. As time goes on, you will notice more and more refinement and standard spelling developing. It is important also to recognize that your child's writing is evidence that she is learning and being taught how to spell.

If there was one thing I could work on to help my child become a better speller, what would it be?

Make time to read with your child at home. If you have time to do a second thing, play word games such as Scrabble, Spill and Spell, and Twenty Word Questions. When you don't have time to sit down with your child, give her paper and colored pencils to write a letter to Grandma or a favorite uncle. Resist the urge to "help" by correcting her errors!

My child's teacher says he should use the spell checker on his research report. I think it will make him a lazy speller. Is this teacher nuts or am I?

Using a spell checker may actually help children become better spellers, as they have to attend to the visual details of individual words to identify the word they meant to write. For "chunk-style" readers, this may be one way of building a mental store of complete visual representations of words. In other words, they have to slow down and look carefully at the details of the word they are trying to spell. Comments from adults who use spell checkers indicate these programs actually help them become better spellers. This seems to be true for children as well.

When do I begin this spelling program? I teach grade two.

We recommend beginning the Wordsmithing program in grade three because by then most children have developed an understanding of the processes of writing and reading and are able to do both independently. The majority of children are at a stage of cognitive development that allows them to understand the relationships among words and how words are used. By this time, they have a basic understanding of the English phonetic system and good sequencing skills, and are ready to expand their repertoire of spelling strategies.

For younger children we recommend lots of word play, exploration, and invention, and many opportunities for independent writing through such things as journals and letters. More formal instruction can be provided through activities such as Calendar and Mystery Message, and by talking about words they encounter in their reading. Some teachers find it helpful to focus on frequently used words, such as *said, they, where, from,* and *were* for five minutes every day. We have also found children who have difficulty with sequencing or letter-sound correspondences benefit from five minutes a day with a structured spelling program such as *Spelling Through Phonics*, by Robert and Marlene McCracken.

What's wrong with the old spelling programs where everyone learned the same words at the same time?

If you think back to our experiences as students, you'll recall some students got 100 percent on the pretest every week, while others couldn't even pass the final test with 50 percent. It is our experience that neither of these groups of children learned anything about spelling from this approach. By holding a common focus for our spelling lessons, but providing different options for individual students, we are able to provide whole-class instruction and still ensure each child will be challenged and successful.

I use the writing process, and I wonder why people would bother having a spelling program at all. What's wrong with incidental teaching of spelling?

Nothing. It's just not enough.

Why would teachers spend time, in an already overloaded schedule, to teach spelling when there are computers with spell checkers?

Even if one assumes that we produce all of our writing on a computer, for a spell checker to work, it has to be able to recognize what the word might possibly be. Writers must still have enough knowledge of the English spelling system to produce close approximations to correct spellings.

How long should I spend teaching spelling each week?

First of all, recognize the many things you do during the day that support spelling development—writing process, calendar time, dictionary work. For specific spelling instruction, twenty minutes a day is usually effective.

Does formally teaching spelling actually make a difference?

Yes, it does seem to make a difference, but only if the focus is on understanding words rather than just memorizing them.

Why is it some of my students don't seem to learn to spell, yet their classmates who receive the same instruction do? These aren't stupid or learning disabled students. Are they just lazy?

No, they are not lazy, but they may be embarrassed, frustrated, and afraid to write because of their inability to spell. While most people become visual spellers who fill their mental visual store of words largely through reading, some people never develop this ability. They seem to be "wired" differently than the rest of the population. It is important to note that there is *no* relationship between intelligence and spelling ability, except at the lower levels of intelligence—levels designated as mentally challenged. For the students who are unexpectedly poor spellers, it is particularly important to recognize their skills and abilities in other areas and not let their spelling difficulties interfere with their success. Many of our best and brightest artists, inventors, and authors have been poor spellers.

Why don't teachers just teach the spelling rules?

"When two vowels go walking the first does the talking and the second is silent," is one rule we all know. Now let's look at some of the words children commonly use in elementary school—*friend, bears, said, neighbor, height, geography*—the list of exceptions is endless. This spelling rule, like most spelling rules, has so many exceptions that it confuses more than clarifies spelling for children. Rather than teaching spelling rules, we recommend working with your students to find common patterns, such as *ea, igh, ar,* and *ough,* that appear in English words. Focusing on spelling relationships based on word meanings, as in the spellings for *sign* and *signal,* also helps.

Conclusion

We have had a lot of fun writing this book. We've learned from the process of clarifying and explaining not only *what* we do with our students, but more importantly *why* we do it.

You, too, have an opportunity to learn and grow with your students. Wordsmithing can add a whole new dimension of enjoyment to the spelling process—an enjoyment that grows out of understanding the English language and why it is as it is. This understanding gives students the tools they need to unlock spelling problems.

We have found that students benefit in ways other than increased spelling ability when they become wordsmiths. Knowing about root words, suffixes, and the relationships between meaning and spelling all lead to a better understanding of the words they read and write. By playing with word families, children expand their vocabularies, which helps in content subjects like science and social studies.

Spelling is not the most important thing a student does, but it is part of everything that he or she does throughout the day. Likewise, spelling instruction should occur throughout the day—whenever an interesting word appears in print or whenever children need help in understanding how to write a word. Give a small amount of time to the Wordsmithing program daily, and encourage word awareness throughout the day.

Remember that just as the anvil is a tool for the blacksmith, spelling is a tool for the wordsmith. Neither the anvil nor correct spelling is the end goal. They are the tools that allow the smiths to carry out their crafts.

Welcome to the world of wordsmithing. Have fun!

APPENDIX:
BLACKLINE MASTERS

Note: The following blackline masters may be reproduced for classroom use. To enlarge to 8 1/2 x 11", please set copier at **128**%; to 11 x 17", at **200**%.

Spelling Contract

Name _____

Week of _____

I have agreed to study the following _____ words from this week's
Class Word Collection.   #

1 _____	11 _____
2 _____	12 _____
3 _____	13 _____
4 _____	14 _____
5 _____	15 _____
6 _____	16 _____
7 _____	17 _____
8 _____	18 _____
9 _____	19 _____
10 _____	20 _____

My spelling partner for this week is _____.

Student Signature _____
Partner Signature _____
Teacher Signature _____
Parent(s) Signature(s) _____
_____

Notes: _____
_____

Page 9: Spelling Contract

Looks Like, Sounds Like

_____   looks like   _____
               but sounds like   _____

[Also works with]
               _____   _____
               _____   _____
               _____   _____

_____   looks like   _____
               but sounds like   _____

[Also works with]
               _____   _____
               _____   _____
               _____   _____

_____   looks like   _____
               but sounds like   _____

[Also works with]
               _____   _____
               _____   _____
               _____   _____

_____   looks like   _____
               but sounds like   _____

[Also works with]
               _____   _____
               _____   _____
               _____   _____

Page 35: Looks Like, Sounds Like

Spelling Test

Name _____ Partner _____

Date _____

	dictated words	correct spelling	checked by partner	number of letters correct / number of letters in word
1				
2				
3				
4				
5				
6				
7				
8				
9				
10				
11				
12				
13				
14				
15				
16				
17				
18				

a _____ Total number of letters correct _____ ÷ _____ x 100 = _____ %
b _____ Total number of letters   a   b

a _____ Total number of words correct _____ ÷ _____ x 100 = _____ %
b _____ Total number of words   a   b

Page 58: Peer test

Name _____ **Date** _____

My word collection for this week

I got _____ words correct on my test that _____ gave me.

I got _____ letters right on my test.

I learned to remember the spelling of _____
by _____

I am proud of myself as a speller because _____
_____
_____

Parent response

Dear _____
         child

I am proud of you as a speller because _____
_____
_____

I wish _____
_____

Sincerely _____

Page 60: Student Self-report

Name _____ **Date** _____

Dear _____

My spelling is improving! I know this because

1.

2.

3.

I am proud of myself as a speller because _____

One spelling problem I am working on is _____

You can help me by _____

My next spelling goal is _____

I have attached some spelling work for you to look at

Sincerely _____

Date _____

Dear _____
         child

Thank you for showing us your spelling work. I/we are impressed by

1.

2.

3.

One thing we'd like you to know is _____

Sincerely _____

Dear _____
         child's teacher

We'd like to let you know _____

Thanks _____

Page 61: Parent-response form

118 **Building Connections: WORDSMITHING**

Error Analysis Sheet

Name _____

Date	Word	Error type							
		Vowel	Consonant	Word Middle	Suffix/Prefix	3C's*	Silent Letters	Meaning	Letter Order

* 3C's = Contractions, Compounds, and Conundrums

Page 68: Error Analysis Sheet

Spelling Focus			**Date**

Page 85: Data collection grid

Spelling Analysis

Name _____   **Date** _____

Checked by _____

The piece of work I'm analyzing is _____
_____

Words Spelled Correctly

1. _____   4. _____   7. _____
2. _____   5. _____   8. _____
3. _____   6. _____   9. _____

Spelling Errors

1. _____   4. _____   7. _____
2. _____   5. _____   8. _____
3. _____   6. _____   9. _____

Questions about your spelling

Q. _____
_____

A. _____
_____

Q. _____
_____

A. _____
_____

Q. _____
_____

A. _____
_____

Page 88: Personal spelling survey

Name _____
Date _____

This piece of work shows _____
_____
_____
_____

The hardest word for me to spell was _____
because _____
_____
_____

Name _____
Date _____

When you are looking at the spelling in this story please notice that:

1 _____
_____
_____

2 _____
_____
_____

Name _____
Date _____

When we were building our Spelling Spines I was surprised to learn that _____
_____
_____

This surprised me because
_____
_____

Spelling Compliments

I would like to give myself the following spelling compliments
_____
_____
_____
_____
_____

Name _____
Date _____

Page 89: Reflection frames

Spelling Profile of the Week

Name _____

Date _____

My word list for this week

_____ _____ _____ _____
_____ _____ _____ _____
_____ _____ _____ _____
_____ _____ _____ _____
_____ _____ _____ _____

I selected these words because _____
_____
_____

During the week I learned these three interesting facts about my words
_____
_____
_____

I had to really work hard to learn these words _____
_____

The best part of spelling this week was _____
_____

My spelling goal for next week is _____
_____
because _____
_____

Page 89: Spelling profile of the week

Spelling and Writing Conventions Checklist

Name _____ **Date** _____

For _____

Criteria	Student ____	Peer ____	Teacher ____
correct spelling			
correct use of punctuation			
correct capitalization			
correct formatting			
neat presentation			
legible text			
Other:			

✔ Yes   ✗ No   **N/A** Not Applicable

See over for procedures list.

Page 90: Spelling and Writing Checklist

Procedures Checklist
for checking spelling and writing conventions

☐ read text forward to proofread and edit

☐ read backward to proofread

☐ read by peer out loud to me

☐ spell checker used

☐ capital letter corrections made

☐ punctuation corrected

☐ variety of punctuation used (: , ; , " " ( ))

☐ handwriting legible/legible text

☐ illustrations labelled neatly

☐ cover/title page

☐ Other: _____
_____
_____
_____

See over for spelling checklist.

Page 90: Procedures checklist

Dear Parent(s)/Guardian(s):

Spelling is important. It is valued not only in our classroom but in the world at large. While some people are excellent spellers and spelling is easy for them, others have lots of difficulty spelling. The key to easier spelling for these students is to help them understand why different words are spelled the way they are. We want to put them at ease with words so they enjoy using them.

Here is an overview of our weekly spelling program:

Monday	Collecting the Words *(20 minutes)*
Tuesday	Taking a Closer Look *(10-20 minutes)*
Wednesday	Making Sense of Words *(10-20 minutes)*
Thursday	Playing with Words *(20 minutes)*
Friday	Showing What We Know *(20-30 minutes)*

Many parents ask how they can help their son or daughter at home. I recognize that, in today's world, everyone is extremely busy and finding a specific night of the week to work with your child is not always possible. With our program, you can select any night during the week to spend ten minutes helping your children improve their spelling. Please try to schedule a few minutes on Monday evenings or Tuesday mornings to read through your child's word list for the week. (These words are taken from our studies this year, with each week's word list having a different emphasis). As well, please sign your child's spelling contract form.

If you choose Monday

Read the list and sign the contract form. If you have more time, you could
- discuss words on list
- brainstorm related words

Page 96: Letter to parents

If you choose *Tuesday*

- help your child focus on the order of sounds and letters in words by taking turns with your child saying parts of the word. For example, with the word *information*, the exercise would go
  CHILD: in
  PARENT: for
  CHILD: ma
  PARENT: tion
- using letters from a scrabble game (or letters on small squares of paper) select a word, scramble the letters, and invite your child to figure out the word and put the letters in the correct order. Then have them do the same for you.

If you choose *Wednesday*

- make up your own systems for remembering words, for example, "friend in the end"
- search out all the ways you can change a word by adding on new endings (suffixes) or new beginnings (prefixes), for example, *happy, unhappy, happiness*

If you choose *Thursday*

- play word games such as Game Over (Hangman with a new name), Scrabble, Spill and Spell, and Pictionary
- give your child a practice spelling test. After taking the test, it is important that your child compares what he or she has written with the weekly list. Together you can both try to figure out why any mistakes occurred.

If you choose *Friday*

- celebrate the number of words and the number of letters your child got correct on his/her test or other Friday activity
- relax and enjoy one another's company at the end of a hectic week!

Thank you for being so supportive of your child's learning at school. If you have any questions for me please do not hesitate to call.

Best wishes,

Information About Spelling Development

Have you ever wondered why some of the "best and brightest" children are not good spellers? Even when they have weekly spelling lists and tests on Friday? Research over the past few years has shown that learning to spell is, like learning to speak, a developmental process. It has also indicated that good spellers and unexpectedly poor spellers differ in the way they think and store information in their brain.

Most children rely on a sounding-out strategy during the primary years—the strategy most available to them at their stage of cognitive development. At around age ten, most people begin to shift to how a word looks and base its spelling on how other, similar words are spelled. This occurs because changes in the brain's cognitive development allow for storage of the visual representations of words. As children become exposed to more and more words through their reading and writing experiences, they are supported in this shift to more effective spelling strategies.

Not all learners make this shift, though, and some make it later than others. Various researchers have suggested that anywhere from 5 to 20 percent of the normally functioning population with average and above-average intelligence continue to be poor spellers throughout their adulthood. Researchers theorize that these unexpectedly poor spellers read quickly by chunking words, while good spellers tend to process printed information word by word. The word-by-word readers see words over and over and develop a strong visual image of how a word looks, while those who read by chunking seem to be reading so quickly that they don't see every letter. Therefore, they can't recall every letter when it comes to spelling a word.

Continued on page 2

Page 1

Page 101: Newsletter

Many inventors, scientists, authors, musicians, artists, actors, and athletes have been poor at spelling. In school, poor spellers were penalized. Their knowledge was masked by poor spelling and they did poorly in school as a result. By making spelling count when it shouldn't, children's achievements in many areas have been inadvertently hindered. For example, if a child is gifted in sciences, it is unacceptable to give an average or low mark because "points were taken off for spelling." If a student can't spell, it means only one thing—that the student can't spell. It doesn't mean that the student is lazy or stupid, and shouldn't mean that the student is blocked from succeeding in other areas of study.

The view of correct spelling as a key indicator of intelligence and success—and poor spelling as a sign of laziness, stupidity, or willful disregard for adult conventions—pervades society at large. People cringe when they see misspelled words on signs, menus, or posters. They become concerned when they see misspelled words on children's schoolwork, and often blame teachers, falling standards, and lack of emphasis on spelling in general and phonics in particular. Unfortunately children are often blamed, and as a result, too many students come to believe that their inability to spell correctly is a sign that they are stupid. Wrong! Research shows that there are other reasons for the apparent increase in the number of misspellings.

In some cases, the amount of children's written work has increased, and their written vocabulary has expanded in richness and variety. As a result these children are making more errors because they are attempting to spell more words. This does not indicate a general decline in spelling ability and instruction but rather a general increase in amount of writing and variety of vocabulary. In other cases children, whose leisure activities have shifted from reading to watching

Continued on page 3

television and videos, and playing computer games, have fewer opportunities to see words in print and develop their visual store. As a result, their spelling growth is hindered.

No matter what kinds of experiences children bring with them to our classroom, spelling is important and therefore we study words and their spellings every day. If you would like to learn more about learning to spell or how the brain works, you might want to borrow the following books from our class parent library:

If you have any questions for me please call. I'd be happy to discuss any aspect of our classroom program with you.

Games to Play at Home

1. Pictionary
2. Balderdash
3. Scrabble
4. Spill and Spell
5. Boggle
6. Wheel of Fortune

Page 3

Home Resources for Spelling

1. Good quality dictionary that contains information about word origins
2. Thesaurus and/or dictionary of synonyms
3. Crossword puzzle dictionary
4. Spell checker on your word-processing program

This week's class word collection	**Personal word list**

Page 4

BIBLIOGRAPHY

Atwell, Nancie, Ed. *Coming to Know: Writing to Learn in the Intermediate Grades*. Portsmouth, N.H.: Heinemann, 1990

——. *In the Middle*. Portsmouth, N.H.: Heineman, 1987.

Bean, Wendy, and Chrystine Bouffler. *Spelling by Writing*. Primary English Teachers Association, 1987. Distributed by Heinemann, Portsmouth, N.H.

Booth, David, Ed. *Spelling Links: Reflections on Spelling and Its Place in the Curriculum*. Markham, Ont.: Pembroke, 1991.

Booth, David, Jack Booth, Jo Phenix, and Doreen Scott-Dunne. *Word Sense Levels A–D*. Toronto: Meadowbrook Press, Harcourt Brace, 1994.

Brownlie F., S. Close, and L. Wingren. *Tomorrow's Classroom Today*. Markham, Ont.: Pembroke, 1990.

Buchanan, Ethel. *Spelling for Whole Language Classrooms*. Winnipeg, Man.: Whole Language Consultants, 1989.

Caine, Renate N., and Geoffrey Caine. *Making Connections: Teaching and the Human Brain*. Alexandria, Va.: Association for Supervision and Curriculum Development, 1991.

Currah, J., and J. Felling. *On a Roll to Spelling…. and More*. Edmonton, Alta.: Boxcars and One-Eyed Jacks, 1995.

Damasio, A. *Descarte's Error: Emotion, Reason and the Human Brain*. New York: Grosset/Putnam, 1994.

Davies, A., and C. Politano. *Building Connections: Multi-Age and More*. Winnipeg, Man.: Peguis, 1994.

Davies, A., C. Politano, and C. Cameron. *Building Connections: Making Themes Work*. Winnipeg, Man.: Peguis, 1993.

Davies, A., C. Cameron, C. Politano, and K. Gregory. *Together Is Better: Collaborative Assessment, Evaluation, and Reporting*. Winnipeg, Man.: Peguis, 1992.

Frith, U., Ed. *Cognitive Processes in Spelling*. London: Academic Press, 1980.

Gardner, Howard. *Frames of Mind: The Theory of Multiple Intelligence.* New York: Basic Books, 1985.

Gentry, J. Richard. *Spel...Is a Four Letter Word.* New York: Scholastic, 1987.

Goleman, D. *Emotional Intelligence: Why It Can Matter More Than IQ.* New York: Bantam, 1995.

Harste J., and K. Short, with Carolyn Burke. *Creating Classrooms for Authors.* Portsmouth, N.H.: Heinemann, 1988.

Harste, J., C. Burke, and V. Woodward. *The Young Child as Reader, Writer, and Informant.* Bloomington, Ind.: Indiana University, 1983.

Healy, Jane. *Endangered Minds: Why Children Don't Think and What We Can Do About It.* New York: Simon and Schuster, 1990.

Henderson, E., and J. Beers. Eds. *Developmental and Cognitive Aspects of Learning to Spell.* Newark, Del.: International Reading Association, 1980.

Jensen, Eric. *Brain-based Learning and Teaching.* Del Mar, Cal.: Turning Point Publishing, 1995.

Johnson, Terry, and Daphne Louis. *Literacy Through Literature.* Richmond Hill, Ont.: Scholastic, 1987.

Kohn, A. *Punished by Rewards.* New York: Houghton Mifflin, 1993.

Kropp, Paul. *The Reading Solution: Making Your Child A Reader for Life.* New York: Random House, 1993.

McCracken, Marlene, and Robert McCracken. *Spelling Through Phonics* (revised). Winnipeg, Man.: Peguis Publishers, 1996.

Morris, Thea. *Jellybean Spelling.* Calgary, Alta.: Jellybean Connections, 1994.

Perkins, D. *Outsmarting I.Q.: The Emerging Science of Learnable Intelligence.* New York: Free Press, 1995.

Phenix, Jo. *Teaching the Skills.* Markham, Ont.: Pembroke Publishers, 1994.

Smith, Ardy. *Cognitive Processes Related to Spelling Development in Grades 5-7.* Dissertation. Victoria, B.C., 1992.

Tarasoff, Mary. *Spelling Strategies You Can Teach.* Active Learning Institute, 1990. Distributed by Peguis Publishers, Winnipeg, Man.

TEACHER REFERENCE LIST OF SOME COMMON SPELLING PATTERNS

IE AND EI

Put *i* before *e*, as in *field, relief, grieve* (Exceptions: *either, height, seize, weird, leisure*)...

except after *c*, as in *receipt, perceive, ceiling* (Exceptions: *weird, leisure*)...

unless *c* is pronounced *sh*, as in *ancient, efficient*...

or if the sound is *a*, as in *freight, their*.

ADDING SUFFIXES

...to a word ending in *y*

If *y* is preceded by a vowel, don't change it, as in *delay/delayed; convey/conveyance* (Exceptions: *pay/paid; day/daily*).

If *y* is preceded by a consonant, change it to *i*, as in *fancy/fancier; pony/ponies; hardy/hardiness* (Exceptions: *shy/shyness; dry/dryness*)...

unless the suffix is *ing*, as in *hurry/hurrying; rely/relying*.

The final e

Drop the *e* if the suffix begins with a vowel, as in *desire/desirable; manage/managing*, but not in words ending in *ee* or *oe*, such as *foreseeable, canoeing*...

or unless the word will be confused with another, as in *singing/singeing; dying/dyeing*.

Keep the *e* if the suffix begins with a consonant, as in *encourage/encouragement; moderate/moderately* (Exceptions: *true/truly; argue/argument*).

Double final consonants

In one-syllable words, double the final consonant if the word ends in a single consonant preceded by a single vowel, and the suffix begins with a vowel (barring special cases below), as in *fat/fatter; win/winning; pop/popped*.

Follow the preceding rule with words of more than one syllable only when the accent falls on the final syllable of the root word, as in *occur/occurred; commit/committee;*

SPECIAL CASES

-ary; -ery

Most words end in *-ary*, as in *secretary, elementary, culinary* (Exceptions: *confectionery, stationery, distillery, cemetery*).

-able and *-ible*

Use *-able* if the root word is complete, as in *workable*...

the root word lacks only the final *e*, as in *excitable* (Exception: *collapsible*)...

the final *y* has changed to *i*, as in *pitiable* (Exception: *memorable*)...

or unless *-ion* can be added directly to the root word, as in *suggest/suggestion/suggestible; deduct/deduction/deductible* (Exceptions: *correct/correctable; detect/detectable*).

PLURALS

With words ending in an s sound (*s, ss, sh, z, ch, x*) add *es* for the plural, as in *gas/gases; ditch/ditches; mix/mixes*.

With words ending in a *y* preceded by a consonant, change *y* to *i* and add *e*, as in *candy/candies; daisy/daisies*.

There is no convention for words that end in *ence* and *ance*; consult a dictionary.